U0107620

托福写作
考试宝典

Bible for Knocking out
the TOEFL Writing

澜大教育集团托福教研组　编

中国科学技术大学出版社

内 容 简 介

本书为托福写作考试备考用书。托福写作作为托福考试听、说、读、写中的一项，一直是中国考生学习的难点。本书基于理科逻辑思维编写而成，总结出了与众不同的英语写作方法，主要包括托福写作概述、综合写作、学术讨论、托福写作常用逻辑连接词、托福写作语法、托福学术讨论模拟题等内容。考生通过本书可以全面了解托福写作考试技巧，提升托福写作考试分数。本书可供正在备考托福写作考试的学生使用，也可供相关教师参考阅读。

图书在版编目(CIP)数据

托福写作考试宝典/澜大教育集团托福教研组编.—合肥：中国科学技术大学出版社，2024.3

ISBN 978-7-312-05869-1

Ⅰ．托…　Ⅱ．澜…　Ⅲ．TOEFL—写作—自学参考资料　Ⅳ．H315

中国国家版本馆 CIP 数据核字(2024)第 054618 号

托福写作考试宝典

TUOFU XIEZUO KAOSHI BAODIAN

出版	中国科学技术大学出版社
	安徽省合肥市金寨路 96 号,230026
	http://press.ustc.edu.cn
	https://zgkxjsdxcbs.tmall.com
印刷	合肥市宏基印刷有限公司
发行	中国科学技术大学出版社
开本	787 mm×1092 mm　1/16
印张	6.25
字数	139 千
版次	2024 年 3 月第 1 版
印次	2024 年 3 月第 1 次印刷
定价	39.00 元

教研组成员

顾问　王　奇
组长　郭晨婷
成员　尹子轩　甘好妮　李媛媛
　　　危　琪　常　宇　张昊凌

前　　言

众所周知,托福写作是托福考试听、说、读、写四个单项中,难度系数偏高的项目之一。其核心难点在于,很多考生会沿用传统的英语写作方法,结果却发现事倍功半,分数停滞不前。

本书编者在过去近十三年的教学生涯中,培育出超过 600 名托福写作考试获得 27 分以上的学生,更有 50 多名学生在托福写作考试中获得满分。即便是在 2023 年改革后的托福写作考试中,也仍有很多学生获得 27 分以上,甚至是满分的好成绩。究其原因,除了托福写作考试的核心考查点并未改变之外,那便是本书编者采用了完全不同于传统英语写作的教学方法,让学生能够快速地提升分数。

这得从本书编者的学习经历谈起。编者自小就极其喜欢数字,擅长发现数字中的规律,数学、物理等成绩都名列前茅。基于这个优势,编者在后续的英语学习中,更是采用了理科逻辑思维方法,从语言学和逻辑学的角度出发,总结出了与众不同的英语学习方法。而这一切,正好与托福这类国外语言考试重视逻辑这一点高度契合。

本书基于理科逻辑思维编写而成,共分为 6 章,主要包括托福写作概述、综合写作、学术讨论、托福写作常用逻辑连接词、托福写作语法、托福学术讨论模拟题等内容,并结合近年来的最新托福真题,对托福的写作方法进行了详细介绍。

当然,本书是整个团队努力的结果,在此特别感谢澜大教育集团托福教研组全体教师,尤其是尹子轩、甘好妮、李嫒嫒、危琪、常宇、张昊凌等老师。

由于编者水平有限,书中难免存在疏漏之处,恳请广大读者批评指正。

编　者

2023 年 10 月

目　　录

第一章　托福写作概述

第一节　托福考试介绍

托福考试是一个由美国教育考试服务（Educational Testing Service，ETS）中心测评研发的学术英语语言测试，托福考试通过考查考生听、说、读、写四个方面的技能，旨在体现考生在学术语言任务环境下的真实语言能力，并可用于本科及研究生阶段的院校申请。托福是 TOEFL（Test of English as a Foreign Language）的音译，指面向非英语国家或地区留学生的英语考试。

托福考试共分为三种，托福网考（TOEFL Internet-Based Test）、托福家考（TOEFL iBT Home Edition）和托福纸笔考试（TOEFL Paper-Delivered Test）。其中，托福家考本质上就是托福网考，其成绩认可度及用途与在考点进行的托福网考相同。托福考试是全球认可度很高的语言考试，被全球 160 多个国家超过 11500 所综合性大学、机构和学院认可，包括美国、英国、加拿大、澳大利亚、新西兰，以及整个欧洲和亚洲，并可用于申请澳大利亚等国家的移民签证。

2021 年 10 月 12 日，参加托福家考的中国考生，需要前往 ETS 授权的香港考试及评核局官方网站购买考试兑换券，即可完成考试报名。其考试成绩同样适用于国内考研、保研及英语免修等，也被广大院校和企业认可。

自 2023 年 7 月 26 日起，托福考试进行了改革，满分仍为 120 分，考试时间从原来的三小时左右缩短为两个小时左右，分为阅读、听力、口语、写作四个部分，每个部分 30 分。其中，写作是最大的改革单项，本书将按照改革后的托福写作题型进行介绍。

第二节　托福写作介绍

托福写作考试简单来说分为两个部分,一是综合写作,二是学术讨论,两者各占一半的比重。综合写作和独立写作的详细内容参见本书第二章"综合写作"和第三章"学术讨论"。

托福考试常规的是线下考试,如今 ETS 也增设了线上托福(也称托福家考),对于写作单项来说,虽然线下和线上版本的题库是一样的,但是设备和记笔记的草稿纸会有差异。

一、区别一:草稿纸

1. 线下考试

考生每人会拿到一张 A4 纸,在开始答题之前不允许在草稿纸上书写任何内容。在考试途中,很多考生的笔记内容比较多,草稿纸不一定够用,所以记得提前向监考老师要,千万不要等听力开始后再要,以免遗漏听力内容。另外,草稿纸要以旧换新,所以考生在替换的时候,记得留意一下草稿纸上是否留有还能用到的笔记内容。

2. 线上考试

家考是允许考生记笔记的,但是考生的笔记不能记在普通草稿纸上。考生需要拿出准备好的白板,用可擦白板笔在白板上记笔记,考生也可以使用透明塑封的纸记笔记。但要注意的是,白板笔比较粗,白板空间不算大,因此,不能像平时在草稿纸上那样随意记录,且要适应笔感。注意,记笔记时要一直处于监考老师的视线内!

二、区别二:电脑键盘

1. 线下考试

绝大部分托福考场的设备不是很新,键盘上的字母经常会出现磨损的情况。考生在时间有限的考场上容易紧张,作文输入的速度会很受影响。针对这个问题,首先建议考生日常多提升打字熟练度,不光是速度,还要学会盲打的技能;其次,坐到座位上准备考试的时候要先看一下自己的键盘,如果发现字母磨损过于严重,应及时请示监考老师要求更换。如果考试途中发现设备不灵敏,对考场设备有异议的,都可以申请让监考老师进行更换,绝大多数监考老师都会热心地帮你解决问题。

2. 线上考试

首先,考生要准备一台电脑,可以是台式机,也可以是笔记本。但平板电脑是不可以的。

对于电脑操作系统方面,苹果系统和 Windows 系统都支持。其次,考生的电脑必须配有扬声器,考生必须使用内部或外部扬声器,不允许使用耳麦或耳机。且考生必须使用非耳机、耳麦的内部或外部麦克风与监考老师对话。考生还要有一个能够移动和 360 度旋转的摄像头(当然考生抱着笔记本原地转圈也是可以的),使监考老师对考生的房间(包括桌面)进行 360 度全方位查看。电脑键盘也要放在桌面上。最后,考生考试全程都要露出耳朵,以便展示没有戴耳麦、微型耳机等可用于作弊的工具。考试的时候要穿得正常、得体,考试是真人监考老师一对一全程视频监督的,且考生的照片会发给投递成绩的学校,所以,请注重仪表,避免佩戴珠宝、领带夹、袖扣、梳子、发夹、发带或其他饰品等容易让监考老师怀疑"会不会是作弊工具"的物品。

第三节 托福写作评分体系介绍

托福写作满分 30 分是由综合写作和独立写作分数组合换算而得的,其中综合写作会由机器和人打分,独立写作也会由机器和人打分。无论是综合写作还是独立写作,无论是机器还是人,都按照 5 分、4 分、3 分、2 分、1 分来打分,打分只存在整数分值。原始分数换算见表 1.1。

表 1.1 原始分数换算

原始分数				转换分数
综合写作		独立写作		
机器	人	机器	人	
5 分	5 分	5 分	5 分	30 分
5 分	5 分	4 分	4 分	27～28 分
5 分	5 分	3 分	3 分	24～26 分
4 分	4 分	4 分	4 分	24～26 分
4 分	4 分	3 分	3 分	22～24 分
3 分	3 分	3 分	3 分	19～21 分

注:1. "转换分数"会因当场考试的难度系数,产生 1～2 分的变动区间。

2. 此表仅列举了部分常见分数组合,并未涵盖全部情况。

第二章 综 合 写 作

第一节 综合写作介绍

综合写作是托福写作考试的第一个部分,考生首先要在屏幕的左侧阅读一篇230~300词的学术文章(共4段)(图2.1),阅读时间为3分钟,阅读时间结束后,阅读文章会消失在屏幕上。阅读期间建议考生将每段的重点记下来,这样便于在听听力的时候更好地理解每段之间的关系。

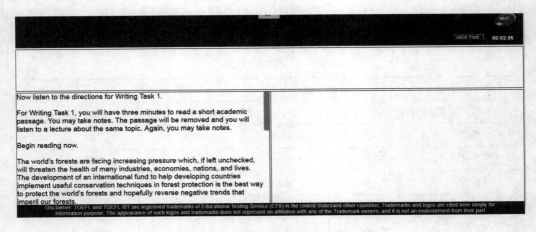

图2.1　一篇230~300词的学术文章

接下来,考生要听一段2分20秒左右的讲座(字数同样为230~300词左右)(图2.2),讲座中的教授就上述学术文章中的同一个话题,从不同的角度提出自己的观点,并给出详细的信息支撑自己的观点。考试中,绝大部分的听力材料是对于学术文章观点的反驳(其中,学术文章会提出3个观点,而听力材料则会针对这些观点给出3点反驳理由)。另外,在少数情况下,学术文章会给出3个问题,而听力材料会依次给出对应问题的解决方案。

Disclaimer: TOEFL and TOEFL iBT are registered trademarks of Educational Testing Service (ETS) in the United States and other countries. Trademarks and logos are cited here simply for information purpose. The appearance of such logos and trademarks does not represent an affiliation with any of the Trademark owners, and it is not an endorsement from their part.

图 2.2　一段 2 分 20 秒左右的讲座

听力播放完毕后,学术文章会再次出现在屏幕的左侧,考生将有 20 分钟的写作时间在屏幕右侧的答题区域进行答题。本题的官方字数要求为 150~225 词,但为在考试中获得更高的分数,建议答题字数为 300 词左右。

第二节　综合写作评分标准

以下为托福写作考试官方指南中综合写作的评分标准(图 2.3)。

为了便于理解,编者结合自己的教学经验,总结出一个简化版的评分标准给考生参考(表 2.1)。

表 2.1　简化版的评分标准

分数	听力细节	语法和逻辑
5 分	全部写到(8~9 个)	☆☆☆☆☆
4 分	遗漏 1~2 个	☆☆☆☆
3 分	遗漏 3~4 个	☆☆☆
2 分或 1 分	遗漏较多关键细节 或包含较多无关内容	☆

TOEFL iBT® Test
Integrated **Writing** Rubrics

SCORE	TASK DESCRIPTION
5	A response at this level successfully selects the important information from the lecture and coherently and accurately presents this information in relation to the relevant information presented in the reading. The response is well organized, and occasional language errors that are present do not result in inaccurate or imprecise presentation of content or connections.
4	A response at this level is generally good in selecting the important information from the lecture and in coherently and accurately presenting this information in relation to the relevant information in the reading, but it may have minor omission, inaccuracy, vagueness, or imprecision of some content from the lecture or in connection to points made in the reading. A response is also scored at this level if it has more frequent or noticeable minor language errors, as long as such usage and grammatical structures do not result in anything more than an occasional lapse of clarity or in the connection of ideas.
3	A response at this level contains some important information from the lecture and conveys some relevant connection to the reading, but it is marked by one or more of the following: • Although the overall response is definitely oriented to the task, it conveys only vague, global, unclear, or somewhat imprecise connection of the points made in the lecture to points made in the reading. • The response may omit one major key point made in the lecture. • Some key points made in the lecture or the reading, or connections between the two, may be incomplete, inaccurate, or imprecise. • Errors of usage and/or grammar may be more frequent or may result in noticeably vague expressions or obscured meanings in conveying ideas and connections.
2	A response at this level contains some relevant information from the lecture, but is marked by significant language difficulties or by significant omission or inaccuracy of important ideas from the lecture or in the connections between the lecture and the reading; a response at this level is marked by one or more of the following: • The response significantly misrepresents or completely omits the overall connection between the lecture and the reading. • The response significantly omits or significantly misrepresents important points made in the lecture. • The response contains language errors or expressions that largely obscure connections or meaning at key junctures or that would likely obscure understanding of key ideas for a reader not already familiar with the reading and the lecture.
1	A response at this level is marked by one or more of the following: • The response provides little or no meaningful or relevant coherent content from the lecture. • The language level of the response is so low that it is difficult to derive meaning.
0	A response at this level merely copies sentences from the reading, rejects the topic or is otherwise not connected to the topic, is written in a foreign language, consists of keystroke characters, or is blank.

图 2.3　托福写作考试官方指南中综合写作的评分标准

第三节　综合写作参考模板

综合写作中由于阅读与听力的结构固定,通常会建议考生整理一个自己的模板,这样便于实际考试操作。注意,模板不建议使用网络上的参考范文,以防被判查重、抄袭等。

以下是一个参考模板,其中阴影部分可以选取同义词进行替换,从而形成考生自己特有的模板。

According to the passage，the author believes that（阅读主旨）. However，the professor in the lecture disagrees，and he/she casts doubts on the arguments in the passage respectively.

First of all，the reading passage states that（阅读分论点 1），while the professor in the lecture puts forward that（对应听力细节）.

Furthermore，the reading suggests that（阅读分论点 2）. On the contrary, the lecturer contends that（对应听力细节）.

Finally，the author mentions that（阅读分论点 2）. Nevertheless, the speaker argues that（对应听力细节）.

第四节　综合写作 5 分范文

一、5 分范文示例一

1. 阅读部分

In recent years，many frog species around the world have declined in numbers or even gone extinct due to changes in their environment. These population declines and extinctions have serious consequences for the ecosystems in which frogs live；for example，frogs help play a role in protecting humans by eating disease-carrying insects. Several methods have been proposed to solve the problem of declining frog populations.

First，frogs are being harmed by pesticides，which are chemicals used to prevent insects from damaging farm crops such as corn and sugarcane. Pesticides often spread from farmland into neighboring frog habitats. Once pesticides enter a frog's body，they attack the nervous system，leading to severe breathing problems. If laws prohibited the farmers from using harmful pesticides near sensitive frog populations，it would significantly reduce the harm pesticides cause to frogs.

A second major factor in frog population decline is a fungus that has spread around the world with deadly effect. The fungus causes thickening of the skin，and since frogs use their skin to absorb water, infected frogs die of dehydration. Recently, researchers have discovered several ways to treat or prevent infection, including anti-fungal medication and treatments that kill the fungus with heat. Those treatments, if applied on a large scale, would protect sensitive frog populations from infection.

Third, in a great many cases, frog populations are in decline simply because their natural habitats are threatened. Since most frog species lay their eggs in water, they are dependent on water and wetland habitats. Many such habitats are threatened by human activities, including excessive water use or the draining of wetlands to make them suitable for development. If key water habitats such as lakes and marshes were better protected from excessive water use and development, many frog species would recover.

2. 听力文本

None of the methods proposed in the reading offers a practical solution for slowing down the decline in frog populations. There are problems with each of the methods you read about.

First, seriously reducing pesticides in agricultural areas with threatened frog populations is not economically practical or fair. Farmers rely on pesticides to decrease crop losses and stay competitive in the market. If farmers in areas that are close to endangered frog populations have to follow stricter regulations regarding pesticide use, then those farmers would be at a severe disadvantage compared to farmers in other areas. They would likely lose more crops and have a lower yield than competing farms.

Second, the new treatments against the skin fungus you read about? Let me explain a couple of problems with this plan. The treatments must be applied individually to each frog. And so using them on a large scale is extremely difficult. It requires capturing and treating each individual frog in a population. Moreover, the treatments do not prevent the frogs from passing the fungus onto their offspring. So the treatments would have to be applied again and again to each new generation of frogs. So applying these treatments would be incredibly complicated and expensive.

听力音频(扫描二维码可听)

Third, while it's a good idea to protect lakes and marshes from excessive water use and development, that will not save frog populations. You see, water use and development are not the biggest threats to water and wetland habitats. The real threat is global warming. In recent decades, global warming has contributed to the disappearance of many water and wetland habitats, causing entire species to go extinct. Prohibiting humans from using water or building near frog habitats is unlikely to prevent the ongoing habitat changes caused by global warming.

3. 5分范文

According to the passage, the author believes that there are several methods that can solve the problem of declining frog populations. However, the professor in the lecture disagrees, and she casts doubts on the arguments in the passage respectively.

First of all, the reading passage states that laws that prohibited the farmers from using harmful pesticides near sensitive frog populations would be helpful, while the professor in the lecture puts forward that this plan is not economically practical or fair. To be specific, farmers rely on pesticides in order to decrease crop losses and stay competitive. Accordingly, if those who are close to endangered frog populations follow strict regulations, they would have some disadvantages compared to farmers in other areas. As a result, they would lose more crops and have a lower yield.

Furthermore, the reading suggests that anti-fungal medication and treatments can be applied on a large scale in order to protect sensitive frog populations from infection. On the contrary, the lecturer contends that there are some problems with this plan. The treatments must be applied individually, so using them on a large scale is very difficult. In fact, people need to capture and treat each frog. Moreover, this medication cannot stop the frogs from passing the fungus to their offspring. In this case, the treatments have to be applied again and again to new generations. Thus, this plan will be complicated and expensive.

Finally, the author mentions that protecting key water habitats such as lakes and marshes from excessive water use and development can also help frogs. Nevertheless, the speaker argues that this method will not save frog populations. To illustrate, water use and development are not the biggest threats. Instead, the real threat is global warming. In fact, global warming has led to the disappearance of many wetland habitats, which causes the extinction of many species. Hence, stop using water or building near frog habitats cannot prevent the changes caused by global warming.

5分范文听力笔记(扫描二维码可看)

二、5分范文示例二

1. 阅读部分

For hundreds of thousands of years of human history, the human brain steadily grew in size. However, about 20000 years ago, the size of the human brain began to decrease. Since then, the size of the average brain has decreased by about 10 percent. Scientists are not sure why the human brain has become smaller, but several theories have emerged to explain the phenomenon.

Climate Changes

Some scientists believe that the decrease in human brain size is a result of the decrease in the overall size of the human body, which has been caused by changes in Earth's climate. Over the past 20000 years, Earth's climate has experienced a warming trend. Generally, warmer climate favors smaller body size; therefore, as Earth's climate warmed, the size of the human body decreased, and the size of the human brain decreased with it.

Agriculture

Other researchers believe that the change to an agricultural lifestyle contributed to decreased brain size. Our ancestors' large brains needed large quantities of proteins and vitamins to remain healthy. After the agricultural revolution, people's diets consisted mostly of grains, but grains are lower in proteins and vitamins than non-agricultural diets. People with slightly smaller brains had an advantage: they were not as affected by the low-protein diet. Over time, they became the majority.

Decrease in Muscle Mass

According to a third theory, the smaller size of the human brain reflects the fact that humans today have smaller muscles than humans did 20000 years ago. This is important because much of the brain is used to control muscles. As humans became less muscular, the parts of the brain that controlled muscles also became smaller, resulting in an overall reduction in brain size.

2. 听力文本

Unfortunately, all the theories you just read are flawed. None adequately explains why the human brain started to become smaller 20000 years ago.

First, the theory that changes in brain size reflect climate changes doesn't really hold up. If we look at the human brain in the period before 20000 years ago, we see that brain size did not correspond closely to temperature changes. Earth's temperature went up and down several times during this early period, but brain size did not decrease and increase as the temperature went up and down. Instead, the brain grew steadily larger and larger, so since brain size was not strongly linked to temperature in an earlier period, there is no reason to believe it's been linked to temperature in the last 20000 years.

Second, the idea that smaller brain size is linked to agriculture. The decrease in brain size has occurred all over the world, including those areas where grain-based agriculture did not appear until very recently. In Australia and southern Africa, for example, grain-based agriculture was not practiced until almost modern times. Yet, humans living in those areas experienced the same decline in brain size at the same time as the rest of the world.

The problem with the third theory is that our muscles are only a little bit smaller than they were 20000 years ago, but our brain size has decreased much more than we would predict from this small decrease in muscle mass. So while the small loss of muscle may have contributed to the decrease in brain size, it was just a minor factor that cannot fully explain the decrease. There must be other more important factors that have caused the large decrease in human brain size.

听力音频(扫描二维码可听)

3. 5分范文

According to the passage, the author believes that the human brain has become smaller. However, the professor in the lecture disagrees, and she casts doubts that all the theories the reading mentioned are flawed.

First of all, the reading passage states that the decrease in human brain size is a result of the decrease in the overall size of the human body, which has been caused by changes in Earth's climate while the professor in the lecture puts forward that. If we look at the human brain in the period before 20000 years ago, we see that brain size did not correspond closely to temperature changes. Furthermore, Earth's temperature went up and down several times during this early period, but brain size did not decrease and increase as the temperature went up and down. Instead, the brain grew steadily larger and larger. Thus, since brain size was not strongly linked to temperature in an earlier period, there is no reason to believe it's been linked to temperature in the last 20000 years.

Furthermore, the reading suggests that the change to an agricultural lifestyle contributed to decreased brain size. On the contrary, the lecturer contends the decrease in brain size has occurred all over the world, including those areas where grain-based agriculture did not appear until very recently. In Australia and southern Africa, for example, grain-based agriculture was not practiced until almost modern times. Yet, humans living in those areas experienced the same decline in brain size at the same time as the rest of the world. Therefore, the change to an agricultural lifestyle did not contribute to decreased brain size.

Finally, the author mentions that the smaller size of the human brain reflects the fact that humans today have smaller muscles than humans did 20000 years ago. Nevertheless, the speaker argues that the problem with the third theory is that our muscles are only a little bit smaller than they were 20000 years ago, but our brain size has decreased much more than we would predict from this small decrease in muscle mass. In this case, while the small loss of muscle may have contributed to the decrease in brain size, it was just a minor factor that cannot fully explain the decrease. Hence, there must be other more important factors that have caused the large decrease in human brain size.

三、5 分范文示例三

1. 阅读部分

The Olmec Empire was an ancient civilization that flourished in Central America from about 1200 to 400 B. C. E. While the Olmec created striking art and architecture, historians are not certain that they developed a system of writing. Researchers have recently discovered a stone block in Mexico that is engraved with Olmec writing. But is it really evidence of Olmec writing? Many experts have serious doubts about that, for the following reasons.

No Similar Objects

First, the stone block is the only Olmec object that appears to signs of writing. When a culture develops writing, the writing appears repeatedly on many objects. But, while many other stone blocks have been found at Olmec sites, none of them have similar markings. This suggests that the markings on the recently found block do not represent a writing system.

Signs May Be Decorative

Second, the signs on the block may have a different purpose than writing. Many of the signs look similar to designs and shapes found on ancient Olmec artwork such as figurines and masks. The designs on Olmec artwork are decorative or perhaps have religious symbolism but are clearly not written language. The similarities of the signs on the discovered block to decorative or religious designs suggest that the block may simply be an example of Olmec art and not evidence of an Olmec writing system.

Origin

Finally, the discovered stone block may not even date from the Olmec times. Archaeologists generally date ancient objects by examining their original position in the ground. However, the block was found and dug up by local road workers who simply put the block in a large pile of other materials before noticing its historical value. Since archeologists were unable to observe the block's position in the ground, establishing the block's true date and origin is difficult.

2. 听力文本

There are good reasons to believe that the stone block from Mexico is a genuine example of Olmec writing.

First, it's true that it's the only all make object that contains riding. But remember that stone objects can experience significant weather damage. The weathering effects of humidity, rain and other factors will often erases any written inscriptions, especially on objects that are more than 2000 years old. Our Olmec block, maybe a rare example of an object that somehow avoid these weathering effects. Maybe the stone was buried in a type of soil that protect it from damage. In other words, many other Olmec stone blocks may have originally contained inscriptions, but on most of them, the inscriptions have been erased by weathering. But since this block may have been protected by a special type of soil, it has avoided damage, and its inscription has survived.

Second, the markings probably do represent writing and not just artistic designs or decorations. When you look at how the signs on the block arranged, you'll find that the arrangement is typical of written language, but not of artistic designs. The signs on the block are arranged in separate groups. Such groups may represent words or sentences. Also，some signs are repeated several times，just like some syllables or words are repeated in written texts. Ordering signs in groups and repeating signs are typical of writing. Decorative designs are not arranged in that way.

听力音频(扫描二维码可听)

Finally，scientists did find a way to date the block. You see，some ancient pottery was found next to the block. Ancient pottery can be dated based on its style，its shapes，its decorations，etcetera. The pottery found at the site had a very specific style that clearly shows that it was made during the Olmec period. Since the pottery and the stone block were found together，we can be confident the block dates to the Olmec period，too.

3. 5分范文

According to the passage，the author believes that the stone block found in Mexico is a proof to show that Olmec empire had a writing system. However，the professor in the lecture disagrees，and he/she casts doubts on the arguments in the passage respectively.

First of all，the reading passage states that there were no similar objects，while the professor in the lecture puts forward that stone objects can experience significant weather damage，which includes humidity，rain. In fact，these factors will erase any written inscriptions，especially 2000 years old. However，the stone block we had may avoid these weathering effects. For example，the stone was buried in a type of soil. In other words，many other Olmec stone blocks may have originally contained inscriptions，but most of them have been erased by weathering. Since this block may have been protected by a special type of soil，it has avoided damage. Therefore，the stone block is a strong evidence for the writing system.

Furthermore，the reading suggests that signs may be decorative. On the contrary，the lecturer contends that the markings probably do represent writing and not just artistic designs or decorations. To be specific，the way how the signs on the block arranged is typical of written language. For example，the signs on the block are arranged in separate groups，which represents words or sentences. Besides，some signs are repeated several times，just like syllables or words. Thus，ordering signs in groups and repeating signs are typical of writing. Decorative designs are not arranged like this.

Finally，the author mentions that the origin of stone block may not come from Olmec times. Nevertheless，the speaker argues that there is a way to date the block.

Some ancient potteries were found next to the block. Ancient pottery can be dated based on its style，its shapes. In fact，the pottery found at the site clearly shows that it was made during the Olmec period. Hence，since the pottery and the stone block were found together，the block also dates to the Olmec period.

第五节 综合写作4分范文

一、4分范文示例一

1. 阅读部分

同"5分范文示例一"。

2. 听力文本

同"5分范文示例一"。

3. 4分范文

According to the passage，the author believes that there are several methods that can solve the problem of declining frog populations. However，the professor in the lecture disagrees，and she casts doubts on the arguments in the passage respectively.

First of all，the reading passage states that laws that prohibited the farmers from using harmful pesticides near sensitive frog populations would be helpful，while the professor in the lecture puts forward that this plan is not economically practical or fair. To be specific，farmers rely on pesticides in order to decrease crop losses. Accordingly，if farmers follow strict regulations，they would have some disadvantages compared to farmers in other areas. As a result，they would lose more crops and have a lower yield.

Furthermore，the reading suggests that anti-fungal medication and treatments can be applied on a large scale in order to protect sensitive frog populations from infection. On the contrary，the lecturer contends that there are some problems with this plan. The treatments must be applied individually，so using them on a large scale is very difficult. Moreover，this medication cannot stop the frogs from passing the fungus to their offspring. In this case，the treatments have to be applied again and again to new generations. Thus，this plan will be complicated and expensive.

Finally, the author mentions that protecting key water habitats such as lakes and marshes from excessive water use and development can also help frogs. Nevertheless, the speaker argues that this method will not save frog populations. To illustrate, water use is not the biggest threats. Instead, the real threat is global warming. In fact, global warming has led to the disappearance of many habitats, which causes the extinction of many species. Hence, stop humans from using water or building near frog habitats cannot prevent the changes caused by global warming.

4分范文听力笔记(扫描二维码可看)

二、4分范文示例二

1. 阅读部分

In 1889, an archaeologist named Cresson presented to the public what appeared to be an ancient Native American carving of a woolly mammoth on a fragment of shell. Its two small holes suggested that it was worn as a pendant around the neck. While some experts suspect the object might be a forgery (a fake), others believe that it is genuine and proves that ancient Native Americans once lived alongside woolly mammoths. The experts who believe that the pendant was truly created by ancient Native Americans use the following arguments.

First, the carving on the pendant is similar to other ancient carvings of mammoths. The stylistic similarity to other ancient carvings supports the pendant's ancient origin.

Second, Cresson claimed to have found the pendant alongside a number of genuine old items produced by Native Americans. These items included stone tools and arrowheads. If the pendant was discovered alongside genuine old items, it is likely that the carving itself is genuine as well.

Third, the pendant has uniform weathering. Weathering is the damage to all old objects caused by long exposure to water, soil chemicals, and other environmental factors. If someone created the pendant as a modern forgery by carving an image of a mammoth on a piece of old shell, the carving would show little weathering, while the rest of the shell surface would be highly weathered. But that is not the case — the carving and the rest of the shell as a whole show the same degree of weathering, which suggests that both the carving and the shell date to the same, ancient time period.

2. 听力文本

Actually, many archaeologists believe that the pendant is not a real ancient object. Many of us think it is a modern fake created by Cresson with the intention of misleading and deceiving the public. Here's why we are not convinced by the arguments you read.

First, it's true that the carving shows similarities to other ancient carvings of mammoths. The problem is that this pendant is actually too similar to one specific carving that was found in France. That suggests that Cresson actually used the French carving of a mammoth as a model for his forgery. This seems likely for one particular reason. The French carving was damaged and the feet of the mammoth are missing. And Cresson pendant carving is also missing its feet, even though there's plenty of space available for feet. This suggests that Cresson copied his pendent from the damaged French carving and did not even complete the missing feet.

Second, let's take a closer look at those other native American items that Cresson said he found together with a pendant. The problem is that those other items are from a completely different time period than the supposed time period of the pendant. The pendant is supposed to be really ancient and date from several thousand years ago. The other items date from only a few hundred years ago. All these objects don't really belong together. So Cresson claimed that he found them together was probably a lie.

And third, the pendant's weathering does not look right either. The pendant was supposedly buried underground for thousands of years in a very damaging chemical environment. If this were true, the weathering would be much stronger than it is. There would be so much damage that we probably could not even see the carving anymore. Instead, the weathering is relatively minor. That again suggests that this object is a modern fake.

听力音频(扫描二维码可听)

3. 4 分范文

According to the passage, the author believes the claim from an archaeologist called Cresson that a pendant was genuinely created by ancient Native Americans. However, the professor in the lecture disagrees, and he denies the arguments in the passage respectively.

First of all, the reading passage states that the similarity of the carving on the pendent to that of old carvings of mammoths proved its origin from ancient times. However, the professor in the lecture puts forward that there are problems with the pendent in that this pendent is too similar to one specific carving in France which acts as a model for his forgery. Furthermore, the French carving was destroyed and the feet of the mammoth are missing. and despite the enough space for feet, the carving of Cresson pendent is missing its feet. Therefore, Cresson copied from the French carving.

Furthermore, the reading suggests the evidence that the pendant was discovered along with some genuine old items produced by Native Americans, which indicates the genuineness of old origin. In contrast, the lecturer in the listening argues that there is discrepancy between the time origin of old objects and the pendent. Other items found together with the pendent stem from a different time period rather than the supposed time of the pendent. To be more specific, the pendent is supposed to date from several thousand years ago, while the old carving found together date from a hundred years ago. Hence, Cresson probably told a lie.

Finally, the author mentions that the carving of the pendent shows the same weathering as the rest of the shell. Nevertheless, the speaker argues that there is something wrong with the pendant's weathering. Buried underground for many years, the pendent should display a high degree of weathering, which indicates we cannot see the carving anymore. But we can see the carving clearly. Thus, this pendent is a modern fake.

第三章　学　术　讨　论

第一节　学术讨论介绍

学术讨论为托福写作考试的第二个部分,要求考生在 10 分钟内完成针对所给材料的短文。本题的官方字数要求不少于 100 词,但为在考试中获得更高的分数,建议答题字数在 150 词以上。

题目的形式是先由教授提出一个讨论话题,学生 A 给出一个观点及解释,学生 B 给出另一个观点及解释(图 3.1)。在考生的短文中,需要提及所给内容的关键点,并提出有别于所给的两个学生的观点并进行解释说明。

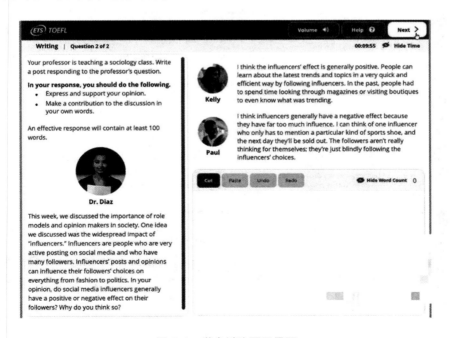

图 3.1　学术讨论题目界面

第二节 学术讨论评分标准

以下为托福写作考试官方指南中学术讨论的评分标准（图3.2）。

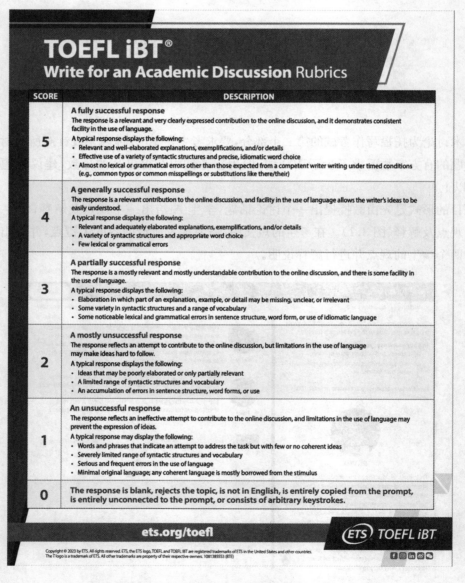

图 3.2 托福写作考试官方指南中学术讨论的评分标准

图 3.2 中的内容此处不再赘述,编者结合十多年的改革前独立写作的教学经验(虽然进行了改革,但是万变不离其宗,核心考试逻辑仍然是一致的),将其简单总结为以下三个评分维度。

一、评分维度一:逻辑

这里的逻辑是整个托福写作考试(不仅包括学术讨论,也包括第二章中讲解的综合写作)的重点。就学术讨论而言,逻辑指的是学术讨论中的逻辑呈现,考生作文中的典型逻辑错误会影响评分的分数上限(此部分和综合写作非常类似),典型的逻辑错误包括但不限于完全重复题干所给的观点、因果关系错误、让步转折错误、并列递进错误等。

具体来说,逻辑错误与分数大致的对应关系如下:5 分对应的是基本不能有典型的逻辑错误,4 分对应的是全文有 1～2 处典型的逻辑错误,3 分对应的是有 3 处以上典型的逻辑错误。

二、评分维度二:语法

语法部分中具体的语法问题可以参见本书第五章第二节"常见语法错误"。但需要注意的是,和托福写作考试改革前的独立写作相比,学术讨论由于篇幅缩短,语法错误的扣分在总分数中的比重会变大,因此语法部分考生需要更加重视。

三、评分维度三:语言

考生经常误以为托福写作的关键是语言的高级性,导致许多考生在写作中大量频繁地使用自以为"高级"的词汇。然而,这里的语言特指语言的多样性。多样性包含两个部分:一是词汇的多样性,简而言之就是要多使用同义词改写;二是句式的多样性,即句子要长短结合,且长难句一定要按照 ETS 所认可的高分语法点来完成固定的高级句式(参见本书第五章第一节"高分语法点")。

第三节　学术讨论阅读技巧

学术讨论阅读技巧主要分为两个:第一,仔细阅读教授部分的内容,找准讨论话题

(Topic);第二,明确不同的题型。

一、题型一:立场对立题型

Dr. Diaz

Over the next few weeks, we are going to look at lots of different materials about the role of television programs and television watching in people's lives. But first, I want to know what you think about this topic. So here's a question for the class discussion board: What do you think is the most significant effect that watching television has on people? Why do you think television has this effect?

Kelly

I know that one way that television influences people's behavior is that when you are watching television, you are not moving around or exercising. This is especially true for children. The American Academy of Pediatrics says that when children spend a lot of time watching television, they have a greater tendency to be overweight.

Paul

I think the main effect that television has on people is to broaden their experience. There are so many programs devoted to nature and travel. Think of all the different places in the world you can experience through television! Last night I watched a program about life in Antarctica, and it was fascinating!

阅读完后,找出不同的立场(即上题中的看电视好或坏),以及立场之下的分论点(即Kelly 的观点 when you are watching television, you are not moving around or exercising 或 Paul 的观点 I think the main effect that television has on people is to broaden their experience)。

二、题型二:立场开放/平行题型

Dr. Achebe

When people are asked about the most important discoveries or inventions made in the last two hundred years, they usually mention something very obvious, like the computer or the cell phone. But there are thousands of other discoveries or inventions that have had a huge impact on how we live today. What scientific discovery or technological invention from the last two hundred years — other than computers and cell phones — would you choose as being important? Why?

Paul

I mean，we're so used to science and technology that we are not even aware of all the things we use in our daily lives. I would probably choose space satellites. This technology happened in the last hundred years，and it has become important for so many things. Just think about navigation，or telecommunications，or even the military.

Claire

I am thinking about medical progress. Like，for example，when scientists discovered things about healthy nutrition. I am thinking of identifying all the vitamins we need to stay healthy. I am not sure exactly when the vitamin discoveries happened，but I know they are very important. Our health is much better than it was 200 years ago.

　　阅读完后，找出不同的观点（即上题中的具体的重要的发明或发现，Paul 的 space satellites 或 Claire 的 all the vitamins）。

第四节　学术讨论审题论点

　　学术讨论审题论点不能重复题干中学生所给的观点。在此基础上，考生再准备自己的观点及理由。具体有以下两种方法。

　　（1）准备一些万能理由，在代入题目前，去掉与题干中两位同学重复的理由，再确定其他理由是否合理，可参考以下思路：

　　当题目中涉及的行为与开口说话有关时，可以用"提升交流能力"；

　　当题目中涉及的行为与跟他人相处有关时，可以用"提升社交能力""有利于适应社会"；

　　当题目中涉及的行为与金钱有关时，可以用"省钱"；

　　当题目中涉及的行为与工作有关时，可以用"赚钱""提升与人相处的能力""交朋友"；

　　其他一些常用万能理由："提升效率或质量""省时""增进和他人之间的关系""带来幸福感或快乐"等。

　　（2）在一些偏抽象或概括性的题目中，联想一个具体的行为或事件，根据该行为或事件去思考理由会更加容易：

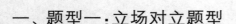

例如：Taking a lot of time making an important decision is often considered a good quality.

对 making an important decision 进行具体化联想：选择哪一所学校上学。

得出立场和理由：a good quality、能作出更好的选择。

第五节　学术讨论基础结构

对于学术讨论的基础结构，需注意以下两点：

(1) 学术讨论只需写一个主体段即可。

(2) 主体段的基本结构如下：

背景引入＋主旨句（Topic Sentence，TS）＋论证＋论据＋论据的结论。

第六节　学术讨论背景引入

一、题型一：立场对立题型

1. 背景句的写法

我部分同意某学生的立场＋分论点概括。

(1) 此处部分同意的是与自己立场一致的学生。

(2) 部分同意指的是同意某学生的立场，但并不同意他所说的分论点。

Professor

Today，we're going to discuss the impact of social media on society. On one hand，social media platforms like Facebook，Twitter，and Instagram have connected people from all over the world. However，there are concerns about the negative effects of social media，such as the spread of misinformation，the rise of cyberbullying，and the addiction to social media use. What do you think? Does social media cause more harm than good?

Sarah

I think that social media has caused more harm than good. While it's true that social media platforms have connected people in unprecedented ways，they have also caused real harm to individuals and societies. Additionally，when people spend too much time on social media platforms，they could suffer from mental health problems such as anxiety and depression. This is probably because they allow people to anonymously bully and harass other users.

Mark

I think that social media has mostly improved society. For instance，it has given a voice to people that previously were ignored. Moreover，it has provided platforms for political activism that has led to positive change. And of course，social media has made it easy for everyone to stay connected to family and friends who are far away. In the past，we had to make expensive phone calls to contact our loved ones，now we can talk to them and send them pictures for free on social networks.

2．背景引入句示范

To some extent，I agree with Sarah's opinion that social media has mostly improved society because it gives a voice to previously ignored people，provides platforms for political activism，and makes it easy to stay connected with family and friends.

二、题型二：立场开放/平行题型

1．背景句的写法

题干背景的改述。

Professor

Nowadays，the world is facing a number of pressing environmental problems，and over the next few weeks，we'll discuss various innovations that may help solve these problems. To begin our discussion，I'd like you to think of one global environmental problem —— for example，it could be related to water，air，land，climate，biodiversity，energy，or something similar. Then explain what you think would be an effective solution to this problem.

Kelly

One of the major environmental problems is the limited freshwater supply in many

25

areas of the world，which means that we need to find effective technologies to provide people with enough drinking water. One solution is to improve the technology for removing salt from seawater，which could allow us to use seawater to replenish dwindling freshwater supplies.

Paul

I think the biggest problem is the air pollution caused by the overuse of motorized vehicles. The obvious solution is for local governments to promote alternatives，like building bike lanes in cities or improving public transportation with electric buses. Both of these would be easy to implement as well.

2. 背景引入句示范

Nowadays，the world is facing a number of pressing environmental problems，such as water pollution（此篇后文写的是 water pollution 的解决方案）。

第七节 学术讨论段落核心部分

学术讨论的段落除了背景引入外，剩余主体结构包括议论文的四大基本要素，分别是主旨句、论证、论据、结论。下面我们将按照完整主体段结构要素进行介绍。

一、主旨句

两种题型的主旨句的具体结构如下：

立场对立题型的主旨句结构：Rather than the previous reason，on the other hand，most people insist that＋TS。

立场开放/平行题型的主旨句结构：From my perspective，TS。

从上述两种题型的结构来看，不难发现，除了一些基础模板的差异外，主旨句的核心部分两者是一样的，接下来我们就来具体介绍一下主旨句的写作技巧。

（1）主旨句最重要的要求是完全涵盖论证部分，如果论证部分是"A→B→C→D"，那么主旨句最佳的结构则是"A→D"。当然，如果再论证其中的最关键成分，则是 D。简而言之，主旨句需要和论证最后的部分完全匹配。

（2）主旨句的第二个要求是正面、直白地完成主旨句，不要采用诸如双重否定类的晦涩

难懂的表达方式。

（3）主旨句的第三个要求是尽量采用简单句的方式表达，避免状语从句等复杂表达。

【例题】 教授讨论话题：Children can benefit in important ways from taking care of animal pets.

选择同意的观点后，主旨句可按照上述标准写成"Children can learn to shoulder responsibility by caring for pets."后续论证部分的最终结论是学会担起责任，因此主旨句中的关键表达则是 shoulder responsibility。

合并模板用词后，两种题型的主旨句如下：

（1）Rather than the previous reason，on the other hand，most people insist that children can learn to shoulder responsibility by caring for pets.

（2）From my perspective，children can learn to shoulder responsibility by caring for pets.

二、论证

（1）直接推理论证是主流的论证展开方式，即正常地把观点讲清楚。这种论证方式的关键难点在于充分性。实现充分性需要做到两点，一是补充前提、条件、定义；二是展开过程，可以将自己放到此情境中，详细描述其过程。这里需要注意，论证过程需要以第三人称视角写，避免出现第二人称等表达方式。

（2）在特殊情况下（即想出论点较困难，需要通过对比的方法进行论证），还可使用另一种论证方式，即对比论证，通过对比"对方不好"和"自己好"两个部分，来得到最终的观点。这种论证方式的难点在于论证的逻辑顺序，"对方不好"和"自己好"这两个部分的先后顺序一定要正确。一般将"对方不好"放在前，"自己好"放在后。在这两者中间加上对比论证的分界线（如 However 之类的词）即可。

【例题】 教授讨论话题：Children can benefit in important ways from taking care of animal pets.

这题使用主流的直接推理论证。我们根据前面的主旨句"children can learn to shoulder responsibilities by caring for pets"。结合直接推理论证的基本标准，将"A→D"的主旨句展开为"A→B→C→D"，即可写出以下论证部分：

Apparently，domestic pets do not have basic living skills. In fact，they need to be fed and be brought out to play at a certain time relatively every day. Though it is the adults who are supposed to attend pets，it is natural that adults are occupied in other business and have no time to attend pets. In this case，children have to perform daily chores related to pets，which requires them to put aside what they love doing and carry out obligatory tasks which are not at all easy ones for children. In this way, children can gradually lean to give up their top priorities for something they must do, which is, in other words, the sense of responsibility.

【例题】 教授讨论话题：Some people believe that people should follow their dreams that are ambitious. Some believe that people should be focused on achieving realistic goals. Which one do you prefer and why?

这道题属于二选一的题型，需要进行对比论证。我们首先选定 realistic goals 作为我们的观点方向，以此写出对应的主旨句"to begin with, a realistic goal would significantly save time for reaching it"。结合对比论证的基本标准，按照"对方不好"放在前，"自己好"放在后的原则，即将"ambitious dreams 不好"放在前，"realistic goals 好"放在后，即可写出以下论证部分：

To be more specific, an ambitious goal is usually ambiguous and immeasurable since the goal is usually so far from reality that hardly would people make a specific plan to reach it systematically. As a result, they may get lost and therefore waste considerable time seeking the right track to approach their ambitious dreams. By contrast, it is both straightforward and motivated for one to plan to a realistic goal. In other words, they could easily achieve their dream by breaking them down into several relevant and measurable steps. Following these steps, they could hardly get lost and march directly to the end, which may save plenty of time from struggling for the right track.

三、论据

对于论据部分，有多种论据形式，如个人故事、名人故事、数据等。需要注意以下几点：

（1）明确论证和论据的差异，简而言之，论证属于观点层面，论据属于事实层面。

（2）很多考生会面临一个问题，在将论证部分写得非常充分后，论据部分无法展开。就此问题，我们需要明确，在论证相对比较充分的情况下，论据相对于对应的论证而言是更加具体的。打个比方，当论证是"对这个房间的描述"的情况下，论据是"房间中的一张桌子"；当论证是"房间中的一张桌子"的情况下，论据是"这张桌子的一条腿"；当论证是"一张桌子的一条腿"的情况下，论据是"这条腿上的一颗钉子"。以此类推，即可明白论证和论据的差异。

（3）若论证部分是直接推理论证，那么直接给出相应的论据即可；若论证部分是对比论证，那么需要给出的是"自己好"这个部分的对应论据。如果论据中既包括了"对方不好"也包括了"自己好"也是没问题的，但请注意不可以只给出"对方不好"的论据。

虽说论据有多种形式，但建议考生选择相对来说难度较低且可以轻松获得满分的个人

故事来作讲解。个人故事的写作技巧如下：

（1）个人故事需要具备的基本要素：人物、时间、地点、事件。

（2）个人故事需要客观可感知，要有画面感，具体来说，若我们要证明一张桌子大，那么我们在论据部分就应该说"这张桌子 10 米长、5 米宽"，即我们在论据部分不能直白地讲出桌子大，但考官可以从中推测出我们想表达"桌子大"这层含义。

（3）个人故事需要注意匹配关系和逻辑性，所谓匹配关系指的是故事的情节发展要匹配论证部分的逻辑，不能存在论证部分环节以外的故事内容，一旦出现了额外的内容就属于典型的画蛇添足。同时，还需要注意故事本身的逻辑性，前后的逻辑必须是合理的，例如，不能出现前文"那天天气非常不好"，后文"我们大家出去登山"这样不合逻辑的故事情节。

【例题】 教授讨论话题：In high school classes, which of the following ways is more effective to stimulate students' interest?

· using technology in the classroom more often
· introducing how knowledge is related to daily life

这道题我们选择第二个选项 introducing how knowledge is related to daily life 作为立场，using technology in the classroom more often 往往会比较难以实现，但是 introducing how knowledge is related to daily life 往往比较容易实现。具体的"对方不好"论证部分就不赘述了，我们直接来看"自己好"以及匹配论据（个人故事）部分：

On the contrary, introducing how knowledge is associated with daily life can be achieved by utilizing articles of everyday use such as beverage and tableware which are universally cheap. Therefore, students have easier access to use the tools, thus intriguing themselves. For example, my high school chemical teacher John once taught us how cola can help to clean our water cup. Then he utilized a bottle of Coca Cola and his glass cup was used to implement the experience. After that, John allocated every student a 200 mL bottle of coke which just cost 50 yuan in total and encouraged us to wash our own cup by it. Since everyone got coke to do the experiment, it really helped everyone participate in it and got intrigued.

四、结论

这个部分的作用为"总结例子，呼应主旨句"。顾名思义，结论这个部分并不是单纯的主旨句的同义改写复述，而是详细地对例子进行总结且呼应了段首的主旨句。根据此要求，结合前文对比论证的示例，可写出如下结论：

Thus, it was quite easy for teachers to stimulate students' interest by introducing how knowledge is related to daily life, such as my chemical teacher's coke experiment.

第八节　不同分数段范文分析

　　为确保权威性,5分范文选取了ETS官方给的真实范文(此类范文并非完全按照本书所讲的结构)和真实考试获得30分且按照本书讲解的格式进行写作的文章;4分和3分范文因无法通过考试分数精准判定考生的独立写作分数,所以选取了ETS官方指南中的范文进行分析。

一、范文例题一

Dr. Diaz

Over the next few weeks，we are going to look at lots of different materials about the role of television programs and television watching in people's lives. But first，I want to know what you think about this topic. So here's a question for the class discussion board：What do you think is the most significant effect that watching television has on people? Why do you think television has this effect?

Kelly

I know that one way that television influences people's behavior is that when you are watching television，you are not moving around or exercising. This is especially true for children. The American Academy of Pediatrics says that when children spend a lot of time watching television，they have a greater tendency to be overweight.

Paul

I think the main effect that television has on people is to broaden their experience. There are so many programs devoted to nature and travel. Think of all the different places in the world you can experience through television! Last night I watched a program about life in Antarctica，and it was fascinating!

1. 5分范文

In my opinion，Paul is right when he says that watching television might broaden your experience. By watching science programs，you can gain valuable insights into new topics. On the other hand, I think that a high percentage of people don't watch TV to increase their knowledge. I am of the opinion that many people watch TV in order to get distracted from their real lives. They watch films or series to be entertained and to forget problems they have at work or in their private lives. At least for me this works well for instance if I am sad, I watch a comedy or a funny soap opera and afterwards, I am in a better mood. Therefore, I think that being entertained and distracted is the most significant effect of TV.

2. 3分范文

In my opinion, television makes the life more interesting and fun. There are so many interesting channels and programs, and they make people laugh during watching TV. I think this is a big effect that television on people, as time is passing by. Especially these days, people lives with the serious problems and accidents. People need something fresh and can entertain. Televisions do these kind of works very well. Through Music program, people can have relaxing time, through comedy program, people can laugh … and so on. Therefore, the television influences people's feeling much better, and I think this is very important effect!

二、范文例题二

Dr. Achebe

When people are asked about the most important discoveries or inventions made in the last two hundred years, they usually mention something very obvious, like the computer or the cell phone. But there are thousands of other discoveries or inventions that have had a huge impact on how we live today. What scientific discovery or technological invention from the last two hundred years — other than computers and cell phones — would you choose as being important? Why?

Paul

I mean, we're so used to science and technology that we are not even aware of all the things we use in our daily lives. I would probably choose space satellites. This technology happened in the last hundred years, and it has become important for so many things. Just think about navigation, or telecommunications, or even the military.

Claire

I am thinking about medical progress. Like, for example, when scientists discovered things about healthy nutrition. I am thinking of identifying all the vitamins we need to stay healthy. I am not sure exactly when the vitamin discoveries happened，but I know they are very important. Our health is much better than it was 200 years ago.

1. 5 分范文

In the past 200 years，tons of scientific discoveries or technological inventions have been shown to the world. If I had to choose one in particular it will probably be vaccine or antibiotics. With Pasteur's work and discoveries，the world changed in a way people couldn't imagine. So many people were dying really young because at that time life's conditions were not as good as the one we have now. With vaccine，we could now irradiate diseases that were killing millions of people，we learn so much about the immune system and ways our body was reacting to pathogens. Medicine evolved so much and keeps evolving every day because scientists are curious to understand how our body is working and how it is able to communicate with our environment. People aged 40 are now not old and still have a really long life to live and enjoy when 2 centuries ago it was synonymous of 80% chance of dying.

2. 4 分范文

From my personal point of view，I think the most important invention is the light bulb. Before it was invented，people had have to use candles for illumination in the evening. Its performance is not very stable，and it produces really high temperature which would probably lead to a fire accident. Light bulbs，however，produce constant and bright lighting at nights. One light bulb could use for several years，which is quite convenient and people don't need to storage many bulbs. What's more，it is safer than past candles. This is a huge progress in technology，and I consider it as the most vital invention from the last 200 years.

第四章　托福写作常用逻辑连接词

托福写作对于逻辑连接词的要求较高,此处简单罗列常用的逻辑连接词,并非全部,可供读者参考。

（1）详细地说:to be（more）specific,（more）specifically,to elaborate

（2）举例:for example,for instance,take ... as an example

（3）并列:besides,in addition,additionally

（4）递进:furthermore,moreover

（5）同向强调:in fact,indeed

（6）因此:therefore,thus,hence,consequently,as a result

（7）转折/对比:however,nevertheless,nonetheless,yet,by contrast,on the contrary

（8）其他:in turn

第五章　托福写作语法

第一节　高分语法点

一、高分语法点 1：定语从句

定语从句相对来说比较复杂，但其也是三大从句（即名词性从句、状语从句、定语从句）中最高级的从句。托福写作评分标准中所说的句式多样性无非就是考生写的句子不能太过单一。对于托福写作来说，根据编者多年的经验来看，托福写作中对于定语从句是有要求的，如果一篇文章没有一个定语从句，那么语言这个部分就会被扣分。关于定语从句有很多内容，这里就不一一展开介绍了，主要挑选一些在托福写作中简单好用的句式进行讲解。

1. 简单定语从句（限制性定语从句）

引导词：which/who/that/whose/where

【例句】

人们都生活在这个科技飞速发展的社会。

People all live in this society where the technology advances rapidly.

这个句子可以出现在开头段的背景信息中。

2. 修饰句子的定语从句（非限制性定语从句）

【例句】

广告可以让消费者对商品进行比较，从而引起商品价格的降低和质量的提高。

Advertising allows consumers to compare goods, which often results in lower prices and improved product quality.

这个句子可以出现在主体段的逻辑链中。

为避免一些考生出现语法错误,因此建议考生,除了修饰句子的定语从句外,其他都使用无逗号的定语从句(即限制性定语从句)。

注意:再次提醒考生,严格意义上来说,定语从句并非有逗号就一定修饰句子,其同样可以修饰名词,但为了简便,此处不展开介绍。

翻译练习:

(1) 有些广告鼓励消费者买一些自己不需要的东西,应该对其加强管制。

(2) 植树造林有助于提升空气质量,从而可以降低患一些疾病的风险,比如呼吸道疾病。

(3) 政府应该审查这些夸大报道社会问题的新闻。

(4) 这就是许多人反对死刑的原因。

(5) 许多员工愿意在那些可以获得晋升机会的公司工作。

参考答案:

(1) It is necessary to impose restrictions on those advertisements which encourage people to buy things which they do not need.

(2) Afforestation can help to improve air quality, which can reduce the risk of suffering health problems such as respiratory diseases.

(3) The government should censor those news which give an exaggerated account of some social problem.

(4) It is the reason why many people oppose the death penalty.

(5) Many employees are willing to work in these companies where they can obtain promotional opportunities.

二、高分语法点 2:平行结构

平行结构顾名思义,即使用 and 或 or 连接的短语,即"*adj.* + *n.* and *adj.* + *n.*"或者"*v.* + *n.* and *v.* + *n.*"的结构。

【例句】

(1) 在家吃饭可以让人们节约时间并且锻炼做饭能力。

Eating at home allows people to save time and train cooking abilities.

这个句子可以用在结尾段表示总结全文中的两个点。

(2) 出国读书可以让人们更好地了解异国风俗和各种各样的文化背景。

Studying abroad motivates people to understand exotic customs and various cultural backgrounds.

这个句子可用于阐述理由。

翻译练习：

（1）使用多媒体工具可以提升学生的注意力,让他们对课程保持兴趣。

（2）一部好的科幻电影可以让孩子获得丰富的想象力和科学知识。

（3）在发展中国家开设新的分公司可以降低生产成本,创造巨大的利润。

（4）技术大爆炸能够对普通人的生活产生巨大的影响,并且可以大大提升生产效率。

（5）这项法案带来了平等的机会和宝贵的自由。

参考答案：

（1）Using multimedia tools can improve students' concentration and keep them interested.

（2）A good science fiction movie can bring children rich imagination and scientific knowledge.

（3）Opening new branches in developing countries can reduce the cost of production and generate huge profits.

（4）The technological explosion can have a huge impact on ordinary people's lives and greatly improve production efficiency.

（5）This act brings equal opportunity and precious freedom.

三、高分语法点 3：实义副词

如果想获得高分,考生必须熟练使用副词,例如"*adv.* + *adj.* + *n.*""*adv.* + *v.* + *n.*"或"*adv.*"做插入语等。

【例句】

（1）我身心疲惫。

I am physically and mentally exhausted.

（2）他极度后悔。

He regrets desperately.

（3）因此,消费者的使用体验增加了。

Consequently, customers' experience has increased.

（4）然而,我有另外一个观点。

I, however, hold another opinion.

副词的使用使得一个简单句变得更加高级。

四、高分语法点 4：特殊句式

1．特殊句式一

Doing … ，句子/句子，doing …（同理，doing 也可换成 done）

原句：When I was walking on the street，I saw my professor.

使用特殊句式后：Walking on the street，I saw my professor.

2．特殊句式二

句子、名词做同位语。

原句：I went to the expo，which was a meaningful event held in Shanghai.

使用特殊句式后：I went to the expo，a meaningful event held in Shanghai.

五、高分语法点 5：难点句式

1．倒装句（部分倒装）

原句：People cannot save time.

使用难点句式后：Rarely can people save time.

简单来说，就是把所有的否定句都改成 rarely/barely/seldom ＋情态动词/助动词。

2．形式主语

It is undeniable that most people pay attention to the environment.

3．虚拟语气

If ＋ had done，should/would/could have done.

如果人们都在家吃饭，他们本可以保持健康。

If people all had eaten at home，they could have stayed healthy.

第二节　常见语法错误

一、there be 句型

易错点：

（1）易混淆句子的主干。

解决方法：如果 there be 之后没有从句，那么不能再出现谓语动词。

（2）be 动词单复数形式出错。

解决方法：be 动词遵循就近原则，需明确 be 动词的单复数，由最靠近的它的名词决定。

翻译练习：

（1）有许多因素和未解决的案例需要被考虑在内。

（2）有一些人支持这项决定。

参考答案：

（1）There are many factors and unresolved cases that need to be taken into account.

（2）There are some people who support this decision.

二、and 并列结构

易错点：在 A and B 结构中，A 与 B 的结构不一致。

解决方法：A 与 B 应该结构一致，如都为"$v. + n.$"或都为"$adj. + n.$"。

翻译练习：

（1）高新科技有助于增加就业和提高收入。

（2）实地考查旅行使学生了解当地的风俗习惯和多彩的历史。

参考答案：

（1）High and new technology contributes to increasing employment rate and income.

（2）Field trips enable students to learn about local customs and colorful history.

三、If 条件句

易错点：

（1）在从句结构（If 句子 A，句子 B）中，容易忽略两个句子间的逗号。

解决方法：If 句子 A 在前，句子 B 在后，两个句子间需要添加逗号。

（2）句子 A 的动词时态或句子 B 的动词时态错误。

解决方法：句子 A 的动词为一般现在时，句子 B 的动词为将来时。

翻译练习：

（1）如果人们可以面对面交流，那么就可以极大地提升工作效率。

（2）如果企业将资金用于技术研发和设备更新，那么它在未来会更具竞争力。

参考答案：

（1）If people can communicate face to face, it can greatly improve the work efficiency.

（2）If an enterprise uses funds for technology research and development and equipment updating，it will be more competitive in the future.

四、定语从句

易错点：定语从句的结构出错，如关系代词（that，which，who，whom）的功能与关系副词（when，where，why）混淆。

解决方法：关系代词（that，which，who，whom）后添加不完整的句子；关系副词（when，where，why）后添加完整的句子。

翻译练习：

（1）你可能会遇到一种情况，使你不得不快速作出决定。

（2）他向受到影响的人道歉。

参考答案：

（1）You may encounter a kind of situation when you have to make a decision quickly.

（2）He apologized to people who were affected.

五、动名词（v.＋ing，即 doing）

易错点：容易将动词原型 do 放于句子开头，导致句子结构错误。

解决方法：doing 具有名词性质，可用于句子主语。

翻译练习：

（1）投资海外市场是明智的选择。

（2）仅仅专注于短期的利益最终会导致失败。

参考答案：

（1）Investing in overseas market is a sensible choice.

（2）Only focusing on short-term benefits will lead to failure in the end.

六、动词时态

易错点：不熟悉动词的时态结构以及时态对应的时间状语。

解决方法：记忆不同时态的结构和对应的时间状语。

翻译练习：

（1）童年时期的经历会持续影响我们如何看待这个世界。

（2）科技进步引发了关于人类是否应该大力发展人工智能的话题。

参考答案：

（1）Childhood experiences have been influencing how we see the world.

（2）With the technology advancing，the topic whether mankind should make great efforts to develop artificial intelligence has been aroused.

第六章　托福学术讨论模拟题

第一节　立场对立题型模拟题

一、Political Science

Your professor is teaching a class on political science. Write a post responding to the professor's question.

In your response，you should：

- express and support your opinion
- make a contribution to the discussion

An effective response will contain at least 100 words. You will have 10 minutes to write it.

Dr．Gupta

As I mentioned in class，governments make public policies to describe their responses to various problems that affect a community. Part of this process involves setting and defending priorities about which issues deserve the most attention and resources. For example，governments need to decide whether they should spend more money on education or on environmental protections. If you were a policy maker，which issue would you argue is more important — education or environmental protections? Why?

Kelly

We all live on planet Earth，and it is the only planet we have. Therefore，we must

take care of it. Clearly, protecting the environment should be the government's priority over education. I think the real question is, which approach to protecting the environment — restricting pollution, regulating population, promoting clean energy, or something else — should be the government's priority.

Andrew

I disagree with Kelly that the environment is more important than education. Education is actually the best way to protect the environment. Educated people can see how their decisions affect the world around them. Also, with better science and technology education, we can develop solutions to environmental problems. Therefore, I think the government should spend more money on education.

二、Economic Growth and the Environment

Your professor is teaching a class on economic growth and the environment. Write a post responding to the professor's question.

In your response, you should：

- express and support your personal opinion
- make a contribution to the discussion in your own words

An effective response will contain at least 100 words. You will have 10 minutes to write it.

Professor

Today we're going to talk about the debate between economic growth and protecting the environment. Economic growth creates new jobs and gives people money they can use to improve their lives. On the other hand, if we protect the environment it can be enjoyed both by ourselves and future generations. If you had to choose between prioritizing economic growth or protecting the environment, which one would you choose. Why?

Alex

I would prioritize the environment. We only have one planet and if we don't take care of it, we won't have pleasant lives in the future. Economic growth can be important, but not at the expense of the environment. I think we need to shift towards more environmentally-friendly economic practices，such as investing in renewable energy and promoting environmentally-friendly technologies. We'll all live much healthier lives if the world around us is clean.

Maggie

While I agree with Alex that environmental sustainability is important，I think that economic growth is the only way to solve many of the social and economic problems we face. We need a strong economy to create jobs，reduce poverty，and improve standards of living. Not only that，but when companies grow stronger and more profitable，they can develop new technologies that solve our environmental problems.

三、Targeted Advertising

Your professor is teaching a class on targeted advertising. Write a post responding to the professor's question.

In your response，you should：
- express and support your personal opinion
- make a contribution to the discussion in your own words

An effective response will contain at least 100 words. You will have 10 minutes to write it.

Professor

Today，we're discussing the ethics of targeted advertising. Some people argue that online advertising which uses personal information to target specific people is an invasion of privacy. Others argue that it's simply an acceptable way to reach consumers with products and services they're interested in. What's your opinion? Do you think targeted advertising is ethical，or is it an invasion of privacy?

Jessica

I think targeted advertising is an invasion of privacy. Advertisers shouldn't be able to track and use our personal information to sell us products. It's not fair to consumers，and it's a violation of our rights. Instead，advertisers should focus on creating high-quality ads that appeal to a broad audience. By doing that they can both increase their sales and show respect for their customers.

Mike

I disagree with Jessica. I think targeted advertising is ethical. It's a more efficient way to reach consumers with products and services that are relevant to their interests. With the money they save by using more effective marketing techniques, companies can afford to offer lower prices to their customers. Plus, we can always opt out of targeted advertising by adjusting our privacy settings. As long as we get a choice, I think targeted advertising can be beneficial.

四、Social Media

Your professor is teaching a class on social media. Write a post responding to the professor's question.

In your response, you should:
- express and support your personal opinion
- make a contribution to the discussion in your own words

An effective response will contain at least 100 words. You will have 10 minutes to write it.

Professor

Today, we're going to discuss the impact of social media on society. On one hand, social media platforms like Facebook, Twitter, and Instagram have connected people from all over the world. However, there are concerns about the negative effects of social media, such as the spread of misinformation, the rise of cyberbullying, and the addiction to social media use. What do you think? Does social media cause more harm than good?

Sarah

I think that social media has caused more harm than good. While it's true that social media platforms have connected people in unprecedented ways, they have also caused real harm to individuals and societies. Additionally, when people spend too much time on social media platforms, they could suffer from mental health problems such as anxiety and depression. This is probably because they allow people to anonymously bully and harass other users.

Mark

I think that social media has mostly improved society. For instance, it has given a voice to people that previously were ignored. Moreover, it has provided platforms for political activism that has led to positive change. And, of course, social media has made it easy for everyone to stay connected to family and friends who are far away. In the past, we had to make expensive phone calls to contact our loved ones, now we can talk to them and send them pictures for free on social networks.

五、Grading Students

Your professor is teaching a class on grading students. Write a post responding to the professor's question.

In your response, you should:
- express and support your personal opinion
- make a contribution to the discussion in your own words

An effective response will contain at least 100 words. You will have 10 minutes to write it.

Professor

In class today, we are going to talk about grading students. Before you come to class, I want you to think about whether grades are beneficial. On one hand, they provide a way to measure students' progress. On the other hand, some argue that grades are too focused on performance and don't provide an accurate picture of a student's overall academic abilities. If you had to choose, would you say that students should be given grades or not? Why?

Lila

I think that students should not be given grades. Grades create a needlessly competitive environment and can make students feel like they are only valued for their academic performance. When students feel that grades are the most important thing, they get discouraged. Instead of giving specific grades, teachers should provide personal feedback that helps students understand what they need to improve and how they can do so. I think that approach leads to more academic success.

Jake

I believe that grades are the only way for students to understand how well they are doing and the only way to motivate them to work harder. Without grades, there would be no way to measure their progress or to identify areas where they need to improve. Moreover, grades prepare students for the real world where they will be judged based on their performance. The only way for adults to advance in their careers is to consistently perform well, and grading children prepares them for that.

六、Taxing Unhealthy Products

Your professor is teaching a class on taxing unhealthy products. Write a post responding to the professor's question.

In your response, you should:

- express and support your personal opinion
- make a contribution to the discussion in your own words

An effective response will contain at least 100 words. You will have 10 minutes to write it.

Professor

Today we're going to discuss whether the government should tax unhealthy products, such as sugary drinks and junk food. On one hand, taxing these products could discourage people from consuming them and reduce health problems. On the other hand, some argue that such taxes unfairly target lower-income families who may rely on these products as affordable sources of food. If you had to choose, would you support or oppose taxing unhealthy products? Why?

Sam

I support the idea of taxing unhealthy products. These products are often high in sugar, salt, and fat, which can lead to serious health problems such as obesity, diabetes, and heart disease. As you said, by taxing these products, the government can discourage people from consuming them and resolve some of these health issues. Moreover, the revenue generated can be used to fund advertising campaigns that promote healthy eating habits.

Tanya

I believe that such taxes are unfair to families that don't have a lot of money. Wealthy people will not care about the taxes and their habits won't change. Additionally，when prices go up，people usually try to save money by purchasing lower-quality products that are cheaper to begin with. If people start buying low-quality food they could suffer even more health problems. There are better solutions to this problem than taxes.

七、AI

Your professor is teaching a class on AI. Write a post responding to the professor's question.

In your response，you should：
- express and support your personal opinion
- make a contribution to the discussion in your own words

An effective response will contain at least 100 words. You will have 10 minutes to write it.

Professor

A new story about Artificial Intelligence（AI）is in the news almost every day. And，of course，companies are spending an enormous amount of money to develop new technologies related to AI. Before next class，I want you to consider the following question：Is AI a dangerous technology that，overall，will be harmful to society，or is it a powerful tool that will improve the lives of people?

Megan

Personally，I think AI is a threat. As AI advances，many jobs may become automated，leaving people without work. That will certainly increase income inequality. Additionally，there's the risk that AI systems could be programmed with biases or used to discriminate against certain groups. We need to be careful and ensure that AI is developed in an ethical and responsible way. Since we can't guarantee that right now，I think it is best to slow down.

David

I disagree with Megan. I'm of the opinion that AI has the potential to solve many of the world's problems, from climate change to disease. Additionally, AI can help us make better decisions by analyzing vast amounts of data and identifying patterns that humans may miss. That said, I agree with Megan that we must ensure that AI is developed and used in a responsible way that benefits society as a whole.

八、University Spending

Your professor is teaching a class on university spending. Write a post responding to the professor's question.

In your response, you should:

- express and support your personal opinion
- make a contribution to the discussion in your own words

An effective response will contain at least 100 words. You will have 10 minutes to write it.

Professor

Funding for education is a really hot topic nowadays, so today we're going to talk about how universities use their limited resources. In the discussion board please respond to the following question: Should universities prioritize funding academic facilities like libraries, or is it okay to spend just as much money on sports and athletic programs?

Rachel

I think universities should prioritize funding for libraries. Libraries are essential for academic research, and they provide students with access to information and resources that they might not have otherwise. Investing in libraries can also help attract and retain the most talented professors, which can ultimately benefit the university as a whole. Sports, on the other hand, appeal to just a few people.

Mike

While I agree that libraries are important, I think that sports programs should also be a priority for universities. Sports can bring the campus community together, even if that just means they attend sports and cheer for their favorite athletes. Meanwhile, among the athletes themselves, sports promote teamwork and leadership skills. Additionally, successful sports programs can generate revenue for the university and boost its reputation.

九、Work from Home

Your professor is teaching a class on work from home. Write a post responding to the professor's question.

In your response, you should:

- express and support your personal opinion
- make a contribution to the discussion in your own words

An effective response will contain at least 100 words. You will have 10 minutes to write it.

Professor

Today, we're going to talk about the benefits and drawbacks of remote work. Many companies have implemented remote work policies in the past few years, and many others are considering joining them. Given that this represents a major change in the way we work and interact with each other, companies must carefully consider all relevant details before making a decision. What do you think? Is remote work beneficial, or do you think it's a bad idea?

Sara

I think remote work is a very positive trend. When we work from home, we spend less time on commuting and we have more flexible schedules. Plus, many people find that they are more productive when they work from home. Some people say this is because they aren't distracted by their coworkers, while others suggest it's because their energy isn't drained during a long and bothersome commute.

Michael

While I can see the benefits of remote work, I don't think it should become the new normal. There's something to be said for the atmosphere that comes from being in the same physical space with your colleagues. I also think that remote work can make it harder to build relationships and collaborate effectively. This means it might limit our chances to earn promotions and raises. And what about people who don't have enough room for a home office? They'll suffer if this trend continues.

十、Smartphones

Your professor is teaching a class on smartphones. Write a post responding to the professor's question.

In your response, you should:

· express and support your personal opinion

· make a contribution to the discussion in your own words

An effective response will contain at least 100 words. You will have 10 minutes to write it.

Professor

Lately we've talked a lot about the impact of technology on our lives. With the prevalence of smartphones and other devices, we're more connected than ever, but some people are distressed by this trend. We'll discuss this in our next class, but before we do I'd like to hear your thoughts on the issue. Overall, do devices like smartphones have a positive impact on the way we communicate? Or a negative one?

Rachel

Personally, I think this sort of technology has had a negative impact on our ability to communicate face-to-face. People are too reliant on text messages, social media, and things like that, which can lead to a lack of nuance and depth in our interactions. It's harder to read body language and tone of voice over text, and that can result in misunderstandings and miscommunication. I think that if people want to become effective communicators, they should talk to people in person.

Mike

While I agree that it can sometimes be challenging to communicate in person, I also think modern technology has its benefits. Smartphones make it possible for us to stay connected with acquaintances and loved ones who are far away, and social networks provide a platform for introverted people to express themselves in ways that they may not be able to do in person. Accordingly, I think smartphones are mostly beneficial.

十一、Learning Styles

Your professor is teaching a class on learning styles. Write a post responding to the professor's question.

In your response, you should:

- express and support your personal opinion
- make a contribution to the discussion in your own words

An effective response will contain at least 100 words. You will have 10 minutes to write it.

Professor

In next week's class we'll talk about different approaches to education. You know, not everyone agrees about the best way for young people to gain knowledge and learn new skills. Let's prepare by discussing whether it's better for students to take classes with a lot of discussions or classes mainly focused on lectures. What do you think?

Rachel

I prefer classes that have a lot of discussions. I just learn better when I'm actively engaged with academic materials and I can exchange ideas with my classmates. When I have the opportunity to get immediate feedback, I can understand things more deeply. I also benefit from hearing about different perspectives and new ways of thinking about challenging topics. Additionally, discussions help me retain the information better since they're more interactive and memorable.

Mike

I see your point, Sarah, but I prefer lectures. I like being able to listen to an expert explain a topic and really get into it. With lectures, there's usually a clear structure and a set agenda, which can help me stay focused and organized. I also appreciate being able to take notes and study at my own pace. I can't do those things if I have to engage in a discussion. Not only that, but discussions can sometimes get off track or become too argumentative, which can take away from the learning experience.

十二、Social Science

Your professor is teaching a class on social science. Write a post responding to the professor's question.

In your response, you should:

- express and support your personal opinion
- make a contribution to the discussion in your own words

An effective response will contain at least 100 words. You will have 10 minutes to write it.

Dr. Diaz

I would like to open a discussion on the topic of social conformity versus individuality. From a very young age, we are often encouraged to "fit in" with others and conform to societal norms, which can result in a lack of diversity and a promotion of uniformity. However, I believe that embracing our differences and unique perspectives can lead to greater understanding and better decision-making. Therefore, my question for the class discussion board is: Do you believe it is more valuable for individuals to fit in and conform to societal norms or to embrace their uniqueness and individuality? What are the potential benefits and drawbacks of each approach?

Ava

I think it's better to be unique and different. When we try to fit in, we often hide parts of ourselves and pretend to be someone we're not. For example, in my old school, everyone wore the same clothes and liked the same music. But when I moved here, I found a group of friends who are into different things, and I feel more like myself when I'm around them.

Max

I disagree, Ava. I think it's important to fit in and be part of the group. When we're different, we can feel left out and alone. For instance, last year, I wore a different style of clothes to everyone else, and people made fun of me for it. But now that I've started wearing more popular clothes, people are nicer to me and include me in their activities.

十三、Psychology

Your professor is teaching a class on psychology. Write a post responding to the professor's question.

In your response, you should:

- express and support your opinion
- make a contribution to the discussion

An effective response will contain at least 100 words. You will have 10 minutes to write it.

Professor Jones

As we consider the role of optimism versus realism in our lives, I'd like to hear your thoughts on the following question: Is it better for people to be optimistic or realistic in their outlook on life? Are there times when being overly optimistic can be harmful?

Emma

I think it's important to be optimistic, but also to be realistic. For example, when the famous basketball player Kobe Bryant retired from the NBA, he didn't just sit around hoping good things would happen. He started a new career in filmmaking and won an Oscar for his short film. So, it's good to be optimistic and believe in your abilities, but you also need to be realistic and work hard to achieve your goals.

David

I agree that it's important to have both optimism and realism, but sometimes being too optimistic can lead to disappointment. For instance, a recent report showed that many people who invested in a certain cryptocurrency were overly optimistic about its potential and ended up losing a lot of money. So, it's important to be realistic and consider all the risks before making important decisions.

十四、Social Etiquette

Your professor is teaching a class on social etiquette . Write a post responding to the professor's question.

In your response, you should:

- express and support your opinion
- make a contribution to the discussion

An effective response will contain at least 100 words. You will have 10 minutes to write it.

Dr. Hernandez

In today's society, people seem less concerned with good manners and civilized behaviors than ever before. On the other hand, if people really want to change the world for the better, they have to risk being seen as impolite or uncivil. So here's a question for the class discussion board: Do you think it is sometimes necessary to be impolite?

John

I believe that good manners and civilized behaviors are always important, even when you need to express a strong opinion. Mahatma Gandhi is a good example of this approach, as he used non-violent protests to fight for Indian independence without being rude or aggressive. However, being impolite can create unnecessary conflict and make it harder to achieve our goals.

Sarah

I understand John's point of view, but I personally think that sometimes it's necessary to be impolite in order to make a change. For example, Rosa Parks was considered impolite when she refused to give up her seat on a bus but that act of defiance helped spark the civil rights movement. Sometimes being polite can also mean staying silent in the face of injustice.

十五、Time Allocation

Your professor is teaching a class on time allocation. Write a post responding to the professor's question.

In your response, you should:

- express and support your opinion
- make a contribution to the discussion

An effective response will contain at least 100 words. You will have 10 minutes to write it.

Dr. Lee

Some young people diversify their time in different activities, while others focus on just one activity that is important to them. So here's a question for you: Which approach do you think is better, diversifying your free time or focusing on just one activity?

Emma

I think diversifying your activities is better than focusing on just one thing. It can help you discover new talents and interests, and also prevent burnout from doing the same thing over and over again. For example, if you only focus on playing soccer, you might miss out on the opportunity to try out other sports or hobbies that you might enjoy more.

Jason

I disagree. I believe it's better to specialize in one activity that you are passionate about and become really good at it. This approach can lead to greater achievements and opportunities, as well as build self-discipline and dedication. For example, Michael Phelps specialized in swimming from a young age and became one of the most successful athletes of all time.

十六、Tuition Fees

Your professor is teaching a class on tuition fees. Write a post responding to the professor's question.

In your response, you should:

· express and support your opinion

· make a contribution to the discussion

An effective response will contain at least 100 words. You will have 10 minutes to write it.

Dr. Gupta

As I discussed in class, universities in the United States have doubled their tuition fees over the past two decades. This has led to students taking out more loans to pay for their education. Some argue that universities should not be allowed to increase tuition fees so much, as it places a financial burden on students. In your opinion, should there be limits on how much universities can increase tuition fees, or should they be able to raise tuition as much as they wish? Why do you believe this?

Tom

I believe universities should have limits on tuition increases. When tuition increases so much, it puts a burden on students who have to take out loans to afford university education. This leads to a lot of student debt that takes years to pay off. If tuition increases were more limited, it would be easier for students to afford education and graduate without a lot of debt.

Jerry

I disagree. Universities should be able to increase tuition as much as they wish. Higher tuition allows universities to have more money to invest in research, faculty, and facilities. This will ultimately lead to a better education for students. Students who can't afford higher tuition can apply for scholarships or financial aid. It's not fair to limit tuition increases just to make it easier for students to afford education.

十七、Tourism

Your professor is teaching a class on tourism. Write a post responding to the professor's question.

In your response, you should:
- express and support your personal opinion
- make a contribution to the discussion in your own words

An effective response will contain at least 100 words. You will have 10 minutes to write it.

Professor

Tourism has become a mainstay of economy in many countries. If a country wants to attract more visitors, it should possess not only a secure environment but also a couple of amazing spots. In order to attract more tourists, which should government do: to improve the safety by hiring more police or to repair old buildings and streets?

Sara

Tourists visit a country for its wonderful attractions, not for security. Nobody will be stupid enough to spend a big sum of money on the flight and hotel to just enjoy the safety of a place. As a matter of fact, some tourism enthusiasts even take risks to visit dangerous places in order to appreciate the breathtaking views there.

Jane

While I agree with the idea that some people venture into some dangerous places for pleasure, they don't seek death. They just want to experience the excitement on the premise of relative safety. And the overall number of people willing to risk their lives is quite small. Truth be told, a place without safe guard and cannot endure life security will not be alluring to visitors despite its astonishing scenery.

十八、Life Styles

Your professor is teaching a class on life styles. Write a post responding to the professor's question.

In your response, you should:

· express and support your personal opinion

· make a contribution to the discussion in your own words

An effective response will contain at least 100 words. You will have 10 minutes to write it.

Professor

City and village are two main habitats for human beings on the planet, and each place has its own advantages and disadvantages. Some people prefer city life while others prefer rural life. Which kind of life do you prefer?

William

City dwellers can enjoy more opportunities to realize their dreams than villagers do. In cities, especially in metropolises, a great many job opportunities are offered, and also there is superior surroundings where young people can carve out their own business. Unlike a city, a village does not have many big companies and a good business environment.

Jamie

I have to admit that there are benefits of living in the city. Still, the living environment undermines its attractiveness. We often hear the people in city complain about the worsening living conditions, as air pollution and water pollution increase. Some even suffer from diseases like respiratory illness, which induces both economic loss to cure the disease and physical pain.

十九、Career

Your professor is teaching a class on career. Write a post responding to the professor's question.

In your response, you should:

- express and support your personal opinion
- make a contribution to the discussion in your own words

An effective response will contain at least 100 words. You will have 10 minutes to write it.

Professor

Career is the source of one's income as well as a way to realize his or her personal value. Some people focus on one thing for their entire life while others try different new jobs all the time. Do you agree or disagree with the following statement? Young people should try different jobs before determining a lifelong career.

Sally

Trying different jobs, young people can find something really appealing to them, in other words, trying different jobs let them find the one which is most suitable for their personality and ambition. But people who only have one job after graduation they may miss the chance to encounter a better job opportunity.

Lily

However, there are some bad influences of changing jobs frequently. Those who often shift their career may be considered as unreliable and unstable. On the contrary, if people insist on working in the first job which they have been doing since graduating from university, they are more likely to be conceived as dependable individuals and their employers tend to favor and speak highly of them, because of their loyalty and concentration.

二十、Jobs

Your professor is teaching a class on jobs. Write a post responding to the professor's question.

In your response, you should:

- express and support your personal opinion
- make a contribution to the discussion in your own words

An effective response will contain at least 100 words. You will have 10 minutes to write it.

Professor

Jobs are of great importance to modern people, which enable people to support their families and enjoy a sense of achievement. Which kind of job do you prefer: the job with regular income and regular hours or the job with high income and long hours?

Vivian

High salary allows one to provide his family with better quality of life. It is because we earn money mainly from our jobs, and money can not only guarantee us decent lives, but also raise our sense of happiness in many other aspects. For example, a person armed with high income is capable of providing his children with high-quality education that can be positively costly.

Mark

While it is true that working long hours generates significant benefits in terms of financial gains, the side effects of overwork are obvious. One will suffer from health problems like headache or even insomnia due to the lack of sleep, exercise and release of pressure. Imaging the scenario that a person lying on the bed to cure his disease has spent all his fortune after years of overworking, will you still feel it worthwhile to work long hours for high income?

二十一、Ideas

Your professor is teaching a class on ideas. Write a post responding to the professor's question.

In your response, you should:

- express and support your personal opinion
- make a contribution to the discussion in your own words

An effective response will contain at least 100 words. You will have 10 minutes to write it.

Professor

This is an ever-changing world. New things keep emerging one after another with each passing day. Whether should people update their ideas constantly or just stick to what they believe regardless of the changing times? What is your idea?

Mary

In today's commercial world, one's refusal of new ideas will knock him out of the fierce competition. With the rapid development of science and technology, every aspect of society is undergoing profound transformation. If someone runs a business in an old-fashioned way, he is likely to be defeated by a newcomer breaking into his field with new ideas. For example, a new way of hailing a cab is gaining popularity with the rise of Apps like Uber.

Jack

Living in the age of information explosion, we are exposed to too many ideas every day, including good ones and bad ones. The new ideas that are radical or contrary to universal values should not be blindly followed. If a person embrace the new idea like self-interest first all the time, people will be in a world where there is no enough trust, dependence and loyalty. In the long run, accepting this kind of ideas will be detrimental to one's spiritual world.

二十二、Courses

Your professor is teaching a class on courses. Write a post responding to the

professor's question.

In your response，you should：

- express and support your personal opinion
- make a contribution to the discussion in your own words

An effective response will contain at least 100 words. You will have 10 minutes to write it.

Professor

University courses can be roughly classified into two categories：liberal arts and science. Both of them are considered as the cornerstone of social development. Do you agree or disagree with the following statement? All university students should be required to take basic science courses even if they are not in the career goal.

Jack

Science is the primary productive force. From the past to present，numerous cases have proved that the world's development is based on the remarkable progress of science and technology. University students，whatever their majors are，will benefit a lot from the basic science courses they have taken. Students of studying science can certainly enhance their foundation of scientific knowledge and those who study liberal arts will be more competitive in job market when they have a basic understanding of science.

Susan

Requiring all students to study basic science courses appears somewhat arbitrary and unilateral because it is not appropriate to make basic science courses mandatory for some liberal-arts students who even have difficulty with their own majors. Mandatory courses require the preparation and passing of tests，which takes plenty of time. Thus，increasing their academic burden will leads to their decreased enthusiasm towards study which can result in the reduction in overall efficiency.

二十三、Gap Year

Your professor is teaching a class on gap year. Write a post responding to the professor's question.

In your response，you should：

• express and support your personal opinion

• make a contribution to the discussion in your own words

An effective response will contain at least 100 words. You will have 10 minutes to write it.

Professor

Whether students should spend all their time on the study is under discussion in the current education. Some even advise students to take a year gap before going into university education. In what way do you think is beneficial or harmful if a student graduating from high school takes a gap year travelling or working before they go to university? Why?

Shirley

Life is not always about studying, and there are other important things in one's life. A straight-A student does not necessarily have a successful career. It is beneficial for the students to reflect on what really want and how they can be competitive in the future, and this needs time. A gap of a year is a good idea.

Karson

On one hand, it would be a waste of time to do this since most of the students are not independent enough to control themselves before they get into university since they are still at a quite young age. On the other hand, when they get to an unfamiliar place for traveling they may risk themselves. What if they confront danger? It is really not a good idea to do this.

二十四、The Manner of Working

Your professor is teaching a class on the manner of working. Write a post responding to the professor's question.

In your response, you should：

• express and support your personal opinion

• make a contribution to the discussion in your own words

An effective response will contain at least 100 words. You will have 10 minutes to write it.

Professor

Since we entered the age of information, creative ability has become an important quality for a person to succeed, and from a larger perspective, it is also a key propeller for a society to make advancement. At work or school, you might encounter a problem that requires creativity. For example, you are given a task to complete that is very different from other tasks you do. In a work or school situation that requires you to think creatively, would you prefer to work alone or with others? Why?

Rudy

When I meet something that requires some new ideas from me, I will keep on working by myself. At first, such a choice can help me develop a habit of independent thinking, which is an important ability since you can't count on others to give you a hint every time. Secondly, solving a problem on my own can be a huge boost to my confidence, so that there would be higher chances for me to make it happen again next time.

Emilia

I would ask others for help if I can't come up with any solutions to the problem I am facing. I confess that there do exist some issues that are really out of my capacity, at least when l encounter them. At this moment, it would be a waste of time for me to continue to think in isolation. Apart from this, it also gives me a chance to learn from others and exchange with others, which also increases the odds of being creative next time just like what Rudy said.

二十五、Advertising

Your professor is teaching a class on advertising. Write a post responding to the professor's question.

In your response, you should:

- express and support your personal opinion
- make a contribution to the discussion in your own words

An effective response will contain at least 100 words. You will have 10 minutes to write it.

Dr. Diaz

We are all exposed to a lot of advertising especially on the internet. And of course, businesses spend a lot of money to create and distribute advertising. Before next class, I would like for you to discuss this question: Is advertising just a way of manipulating people to buy things they do not need or is it an important source of information that helps people make informed consumer decisions?

Karen

I don't think most people consider ads to be valuable. I read that in just one year from 2018 to 2019 the number of computers, tablets and mobile phones using ad blockers increased from 142 million to 615 million.

Brad

People can find out a lot about products from advertising. There's plenty of evidence that people usually begin the process of making a big purchase by looking at ads and reviews. I have to go to another class right now, but I'm going to post later about an advertisement that gave me a lot of useful information.

二十六、Learning Skills

Your professor is teaching a class on learning skills. Write a post responding to the professor's question.

In your response, you should:

- express and support your personal opinion
- make a contribution to the discussion in your own words

An effective response will contain at least 100 words. You will have 10 minutes to write it.

Dr. Gupta

In a recent study, it was discovered that many university students do not have good learning habits. Some think they should be required to take courses teaching learning skills, while others think there is no need to set the classes as compulsory courses. What do you think?

Paul

I believe that university students should be required to take courses teaching learning skills. Learning how to study efficiently and effectively is crucial for success in university and beyond. Without proper learning habits, students may struggle to keep up with the workload and may not reach their academic potential. Therefore, it is important for universities to provide students with the necessary tools and skills to succeed.

Claire

I think that making courses teaching learning skills compulsory is not necessary. While it is true that many students struggle with their studies in university, forcing them to take courses they may not be interested in or see the value in will not necessarily solve the problem. It may even cause more disengagement and resentment towards the education system.

二十七、Celebrities

Your professor is teaching a class on celebrities. Write a post responding to the professor's question.

In your response, you should:

- express and support your personal opinion
- make a contribution to the discussion in your own words

An effective response will contain at least 100 words. You will have 10 minutes to write it.

Professor

Celebrities, such as actors, musicians, and athletes, sometimes express their political views in public. Some people appreciate knowing the political views of celebrities. Others think it is not appropriate or useful to know the political views of celebrities. Which opinion do you agree with?

Shirley

Personally, I appreciate knowing the political views of celebrities. Whether we like it or not, celebrities have a lot of influence over the general public. Their fans look up to them and respect their opinions. By expressing their political views, celebrities have the power to educate their fans and inspire them to take action on important social issues. In this way, knowing the political views of celebrities can bring about positive change and promote meaningful discussions.

Karson

I disagree with Shirley's viewpoint. I believe that it is not appropriate or useful to know the political views of celebrities. Celebrities are not experts in political matters, and their opinions may be biased or misinformed. People should form their own opinions based on reliable sources and research, rather than blindly following the opinions of celebrities. Moreover, celebrities should focus on their profession and avoid getting involved in politics, as it may distract them from their work and tarnish their reputation. Therefore, it is not beneficial to know the political views of celebrities.

二十八、Working

Your professor is teaching a class on working. Write a post responding to the professor's question.

In your response, you should:
- express and support your personal opinion
- make a contribution to the discussion in your own words

An effective response will contain at least 100 words. You will have 10 minutes to write it.

Mr. Smith

Today we'll discuss the benefits and drawbacks of working remotely. Working remotely can increase productivity and offer flexibility, but it can also cause feelings of isolation and hinder collaboration. What do you think? Do you prefer working remotely or in a traditional office environment? Why?

Sam

I prefer working in a traditional office environment. While remote work can be convenient, it's difficult to form personal relationships with colleagues and to collaborate effectively on projects. I think people work best when they can bounce ideas off one another and work together towards a common goal.

Ally

I disagree with Sam. I think working remotely is great. You can avoid the stress of commuting, set your own schedule, and work in a comfortable environment that suits you. Plus, with today's communication technologies, it's easy to stay in touch with your colleagues and collaborate with them even when you're not in the same place.

二十九、Literary Devices

Your professor is teaching a class on literary devices. Write a post responding to the professor's question.

In your response, you should:

· express and support your personal opinion

· make a contribution to the discussion in your own words

An effective response will contain at least 100 words. You will have 10 minutes to write it.

Mr. Barkley

We've been studying different literary devices such as symbolism, foreshadowing, and irony. I'd like to know what you think about the use of these devices in literature. Do you think that using these devices enhances the reading experience? Why or why not?

Kris

I think that the use of literary devices can make a text more engaging and thought-provoking. Symbolism, for example can help to deepen the meaning of a story. while irony can help to create a sense of surprise or tension. I think that these devices add richness and complexity to literature that makes it more rewarding to read.

Mohammed

While I agree that literary devices can make a text more interesting, I also think that sometimes they can be overused or distracting. Sometimes authors try to be too clever with their use of symbolism or foreshadowing, and it can take away from the enjoyment of the story. I think it's important to strike a balance between using literary devices effectively and not letting them overshadow the story itself.

三十、Art

Your professor is teaching a class on art. Write a post responding to the professor's question.

In your response, you should:
- express and support your personal opinion
- make a contribution to the discussion in your own words

An effective response will contain at least 100 words. You will have 10 minutes to write it.

Dr. Bianchi

Today, we'll discuss the role of art in society. Some argue that art is only for entertainment, while others believe that it has a deeper purpose in expressing human emotions and experiences. What do you think? Is art just for entertainment, or does it have a greater purpose in society?

Susan

I think that art is not only for entertainment, but also for expressing and exploring our emotions and experiences. Art can be a powerful tool for social and political commentary, and it can inspire people to think differently and consider different perspectives. For example, music can be a way for people to express their feelings about social and political issues and it can inspire people to take action and make a difference.

Alex

I understand what Susan is saying, but I think that entertainment is an important function of art. People need to have a break from the stresses of their daily lives, and art provides an opportunity for relaxation and enjoyment. Also, some people don't have access to formal education or intellectual pursuits, but they can still appreciate and enjoy art, so I think that entertainment is an important aspect of art in society.

三十一、Choosing the Major

Your professor is teaching a class on choosing the major. Write a post responding to

the professor's question.

In your response you should:

· express and support your personal opinion

· make a contribution to the discussion in your own words

An effective response will contain at least 100 words. You will have 10 minutes to write.

Mr. Pearson

Today, we are going to discuss the choice of major when students get into university or college. Being completely free when choosing a major becomes a trend among students, which means they can base on their interests and desires to choose a major, but some parents will persuade their children to choose certain majors that are competitive and have potential to earn more money. What do you think? Is it better to choose a major based on interests and desires than a major that is promising in the future?

Alex

Personally, I would choose a major that I'm interested in because it's the only way that I am able to find my passion. Without passion, everything I learned becomes meaningless and time-wasting. I think all students should have the freedom to choose their majors.

Joanna

I disagree with Alex. I think students are not experienced and lack the information of society. Under this circumstance, some may even regret about their choices. Why not let parents take charge of their children's study and make the best choice of their majors?

三十二、Taking Photos

Your professor is teaching a class on taking photos. Write a post responding to the professor's question.

In your response, you should:

· express and support your personal opinion

· make a contribution to the discussion in your own words

An effective response will contain at least 100 words. You will have 10 minutes to write.

Mr. Johnson

Guys，here we have an interesting topic on taking photos. We all have experiences on attending big events，right? Such as graduation and wedding. Do you think it is acceptable that people should be allowed to take photos and videos as many as they want? Or is it better to have some restraints to limit the behavior of recording on their smartphones? Why do you think of that?

Joseph

Of course，people should be able to take photos as many as they want. I've taken thousands of photos on big events and no one has yet to stop me from doing that. It seems that everyone is okay with that behavior.

Marry

Joseph's opinion on taking photos is too naive. Personally，I am not a big fan of taking photos. I would feel unhappy if someone takes a photo that has me. It's the personal privacy that everyone should respect. Plus，we can have a good time without smartphones.

三十三、Advertisements

Your professor is teaching a class on advertisements. Write a post responding to the professor's question.

In your response，you should：
- express and support your personal opinion
- make a contribution to the discussion in your own words

An effective response will contain at least 100 words. You will have 10 minutes to write.

Mr. Andrew

Since we have already discovered the mystery of business，today we will discuss an important part of business — advertising. There are different kinds of advertising，for example，commercial advertisements on TV，billboards beside the highway. Do you think that all companies should at least have one of kinds of advertising or is it unnecessary to put amount of money on advertising?

William

I think it's pretty obvious that every company should invest on advertising. I mean I had several experiences on buying something on TV just because I saw their advertising. It's quite persuasive. I don't know how much money that companies made through advertisements, but it is a useful method.

Taylor

There's a lot we have to consider when it comes to advertising. For me, I just don't like seeing advertisements when I am fully focused on doing something, because it's vert distractive. Plus, what if the quality of product becomes unstable or even decreased? Consumers will lose their interest on it whether or not it has great advertising.

三十四、Computer Science

Your professor is teaching a class on computer science. Write a post responding to the professor's question.

In your response, you should:

• express and support your personal opinion

• make a contribution to the discussion in your own words

An effective response will contain at least 100 words. You will have 10 minutes to write.

Professor Wolfson

We all know that there are some popular majors that countless students want to take when they enter universities. Clearly, computer science, being your major, seems to be the top 3 major. We also need to think more about the future. As technology advances with an unbelievable spend, computer science may face a trend of decline in the next 20 years. What is your opinion? Is computer science still popular major in the future or it will be replaced by others?

Jane

This is an easy question. Computer science，in the past，nowadays，and in the future is certainly the mainstream. Human cannot live without computers，and they have already played a significant role in people's life. As long as the world needs computers，computer science will always exert a positive impact on people.

George

Jane's opinion is not very persuasive. There are so many instances about how computers failed people. For me，if I do something that is extremely important，I will not trust computers，instead，doing it by own hands seems to be trustworthy.

三十五、The Market

Your professor is teaching a class on the market. Write a post responding to the professor's question.

In your response，you should：
- express and support your personal opinion
- make a contribution to the discussion in your own words

An effective response will contain at least 100 words. You will have 10 minutes to write it.

Mr. Jackson

According to principles of economics，governments have different ways to intervene the market so as to make an equilibrium. However，some businessmen feel uncomfortable about this and claim that governments should stay out of the market. They also say that some products that are good in some features has been turned down from releasing into the market. It is regrettable. Do you think that governments should intervene with the market and make some restraints on some firms or stay out of the market?

Thomas

It is very considerate that governments pay attention to the market. Without their protection，consumers will face unfairness. For example，consumers pay a great amount of money and get an ordinary product. Forcing these companies to make a change in their price and give a fair price is highly appreciated.

Phoebe

I disagree with Thomas' perspective. Yes，it's true that governments bring us some benefits. But everything has its drawbacks. Last time，I was shopping in the mall and trying to buy a latest mobile phone. Then I was told because of some unspeakable reasons，they don't sell the phone anymore！

三十六、Spare Time

Your professor is teaching a class on spare time. Write a post responding to the professor's question.

In your response，you should：

- express and support your personal opinion
- make a contribution to the discussion in your own words

An effective response will contain at least 100 words. You will have 10 minutes to write it.

Mr. Michael

University students sometimes have free time during the night. Some of them prefer to do some community activities such as being a librarian or a volunteer helping others. There are also some other students devote themselves into a part-time job so as to make some extra money. In your mind，what is the better way to do in the spare time，community activities or part-time jobs？

Mike

Personally，I would like to have a part-time job because I have to consider my career life. After graduation，it is no doubt that I would have an internship first. Having a part-time job not only allows me to make some money，but also offers a great chance to have some real-work experience.

Angela

I understand why Mike said that，but I think maybe it's not the whole picture. A part-time job may not be easy to find，and as long as you are not experienced，no one is

willing to take you as an intern. Community activities can also give you some work experience. It's easy to sign up for.

第二节 立场开放/平行题型模拟题

一、Science

Your professor is teaching a class on science. Write a post responding to the professor's question.

In your response，you should：

- express and support your personal opinion
- make a contribution to the discussion in your own words

An effective response will contain at least 100 words. You will have 10 minutes to write it.

Dr. Achebe

When people are asked about the most important discoveries or inventions made in the last two hundred years，they usually mention something very obvious，like the computer or the cell phone. But there are thousands of other discoveries or inventions that have had a huge impact on how we live today. What scientific discovery or technological invention from the last two hundred years — other than computers and cell phones — would you choose as being important? Why?

Paul

I mean，we're so used to science and technology that we are not even aware of all the things we use in our daily lives. I would probably choose space satellites. This technology happened in the last hundred years，and it has become important for so many things. Just think about navigation，or telecommunications，or even the military.

Claire

I am thinking about medical progress. Like, for example, when scientists discovered things about healthy nutrition. I am thinking of identifying all the vitamins we need to stay healthy. I am not sure exactly when the vitamin discoveries happened, but I know they are very important. Our health is much better than it was 200 years ago.

二、Medical Care

Your professor is teaching a class on medical care. Write a post responding to the professor's question.

In your response, you should:

- express and support your personal opinion
- make a contribution to the discussion in your own words

An effective response will contain at least 100 words. You will have 10 minutes to write it.

Professor

Life expectancies are increasing all over the world nowadays. Some of you probably know someone who is more than 100 years old. Before our next class, I want you to consider the following question: What factors do you think have contributed to the increase in life expectancy? Is it due to advances in medical technology, improvements in government services, changes in lifestyle habits, or something else entirely?

Lisa

I think the main reason why people are living longer nowadays is recent advances in medical technology. Modern medicine has enabled us to better treat and manage chronic illnesses, and there have been major breakthroughs in areas such as cancer treatment and organ transplantation. As a result, people are able to live longer with diseases that may have been fatal in the past. Not only that, but they can live more rewarding and fulfilling lives.

John

While medical technology has certainly played a role, I think improvements in government services have been just as important. We now have access to clean drinking water，sanitation systems，and free vaccines that have dramatically reduced health problems. In the past，people didn't have access to any of these things. Additionally，public health campaigns have helped educate people about healthy habits such as exercise，healthy eating，and about the danger of smoking.

三、Education System

Your professor is teaching a class on education system. Write a post responding to the professor's question.

In your response，you should：
- express and support your personal opinion
- make a contribution to the discussion in your own words

An effective response will contain at least 100 words. You will have 10 minutes to write it.

Professor

Next week，we're going to spend a lot of time in class discussing whether the current education system can help students in their future learning paths. Before we start talking about that in class，I want to hear what you think about the topic. So，here's a question for the class discussion board： In your opinion，what are beneficial for students' academic success?

Alex

I believe that homework can improve students' achievement in terms of improved grades，test results，and the likelihood to attend college. For example，a research published in the *High School Journal* indicated that students who spent between 31 and 90 minutes each day on homework scored about 40 points higher on the SAT-Mathematics subtest than their peers，who reported spending no time on homework each day，on average.

Jack

I think that standardized tests offer an objective measurement of education and a good metric to gauge areas for improvement. In this case，it can give students a strong motivation to learn and examine their own shortcomings. This will definitely make them better in studying or other fields.

四、Study

Your professor is teaching a class on study. Write a post responding to the professor's question.

In your response, you should:

· express and support your personal opinion

· make a contribution to the discussion in your own words

An effective response will contain at least 100 words. You will have 10 minutes to write it.

Professor

Parents hold great expectation to their children, so they would greatly love to help their children, especially their study. What is the best way for parents to help their children with their study?

Sabrina

I believe that parental help with children's homework is necessary. In fact, whenever an assignment can be potentially dangerous, then it becomes parents' duty to provide the necessary assistance to ensure safety. For example, a geography class may ask students to make a model volcano. Parents can show their children how to mix the baking soda to make the volcano erupt, boil glue over the stove to make the paper mache volcano, and use a knife to carve out various cardboard figurines running away from the lava.

Jerry

I think encouraging children to do their work independently helps boost their confidence. If children have no one to rely on, they have to try to figure out any problems they encounter on their own. With their problem-solving skills sharpened and independent thinking improved, children will definitely develop the confidence of their being able to take care of themselves.

五、Environment

Your professor is teaching a class on environment. Write a post responding to the professor's question.

In your response, you should:

- express and support your personal opinion
- make a contribution to the discussion in your own words

An effective response will contain at least 100 words. You will have 10 minutes to write it.

Professor

What is the most important action for the government to solve environmental problems?

Melanie

I really think that governments need to invest in the funding of research and development of sustainable and clean energy sources such as solar and wind power. Today, environmental problems occupy prime time on television and take up many column inches in newspapers. Though there are numerous environmental issues that raise concern, many seemed to be linked to the burning of fossil fuels.

Andy

Well, I consider that humans, by nature, are self-centered and would not hesitate for a minute to cut down a tree or kill an animal for their own interests, regardless of the disastrous effects on wild species and the forest. So governments definitely have to take actions to limit people's wrong behavior.

六、Parents and Children

Your professor is teaching a class on parents and children. Write a post responding to the professor's question.

In your response, you should:

- express and support your personal opinion

- make a contribution to the discussion in your own words

An effective response will contain at least 100 words. You will have 10 minutes to write it.

Professor

Currently, in order to develop children's independence and get them prepared for the future life, many parents try to find some ways to meet these goals. What do you think is the most effective way to help children get ready for their future life?

Tom

I think children can broaden their horizon by taking part-time jobs. If teenagers work part-time, they may confront a variety of headache situations, and in order to overcome them and finish the jobs successfully, children are required to obtain relevant knowledge and skills. As a result, their scope of knowledge can be enlarged greatly. Taking myself for example, I once took a part-time job in a cosmetics company and was assigned to hand out flyers. Though it appeared a simple task, I still learned a lot from it, including how to deal with people and how to distinguish my targets from a big crowd.

Mary

I believe sports is a good way to cultivate students' comprehensive abilities. Exercise can build personal resilience to deal with later life adversities. For instance, my father is a seasoned athlete who never gets frustrated and disappointed when faced with life's difficult problems and always keeps a positive attitude. I think this has a lot to do with his sports career.

七、Choosing Lecture

Your professor is teaching a class on choosing lecture. Write a post responding to the professor's question.

In your response, you should:

- express and support your personal opinion
- make a contribution to the discussion in your own words

An effective response will contain at least 100 words. You will have 10 minutes to write it.

Professor

Various lectures are part of university curriculum，and students are required to study them for credits. Most students are confused about choosing the type of lecture. What type of lecture do you think will attract the most students to attend?

Jane

I think history lectures can bring one's perspective to a higher level. Even though ancient people lived in an age very different from today，the way they acted and thought can still be applied to all aspects of modern life. And therefore，understanding what they did and how they looked at issues is of great significance to us. For example，my father is a successful business leader. Once he told me that doing business was like fighting a battle，and the way he managed his team，how he won negotiations with business partners were derived from his interest in studying classic cases of ancient wars.

Andrew

I believe politics-related lectures can help us to be more aware of our country's status，advantages and disadvantages in the world，so as to help us to be more aware of how to choose a country or a career to work in later. And the world is a community，we need to know more about the respective cultures and pillar industries of each country to broaden our horizons.

八、Life

Your professor is teaching a class on life. Write a post responding to the professor's question.

In your response，you should：

· express and support your personal opinion

· make a contribution to the discussion in your own words

An effective response will contain at least 100 words. You will have 10 minutes to write it.

Professor

As society is developing by leaps and bounds, tremendous changes have taken place in people's life. What makes life easier now than it used to be?

Tony

I think modern communication technology has reshaped our lives and brought us much convenience. To be more specific, with the wide application of smart phones and Internet, it is possible for people to contact each other more conveniently and efficiently. For example, Lily, one of my best friends, is lucky to be admitted to a famous university in America, which means we cannot hang out together like before. But thanks to the modern communication technology, we still keep in frequent touch with each other on Skype anytime, anywhere. Therefore, it feels like we have never been apart.

Ben

I think a variety of means of transportation makes it efficient and comfortable for people to move around. Subways, taxis, private cars, and airplanes shorten the distance between places. My grandparents, who live in suburbs, are good examples in point. When they felt like going to the urban center, it usually took them more than one hour in the past, because of the bumpy roads and low-efficient vehicles. But nowadays, with great improvement of road condition and advanced means of transportation, they only have to spend at most 20 minutes traveling from home to the city. In scorching summers, passengers can enjoy cool fresh air inside vehicles equipped with air-conditioner, which makes the trip very comfortable.

九、Decision

Your professor is teaching a class on decision. Write a post responding to the professor's question.

In your response, you should:

• express and support your personal opinion

• make a contribution to the discussion in your own words

An effective response will contain at least 100 words. You will have 10 minutes to write it.

Professor

When it comes to purchasing expensive good, people are inclined to think twice. They may be influenced by different factors. What do you think is the most influential factor that can make people make a choice?

Peter

I think friends' advice will help me make a final decision. when giving us information about a certain product, our friends or colleagues tend to share with us their true feelings about it. For example, if I plan to purchase a car in an automobile 4S shop, the salesperson will usually lure me into buying a more expensive one with all kinds of coupons and gifts. However, if I resort to a friend who knows cars well, he will guide me to buy the one much suitable for my situation.

Grey

I think the publicity of the mass media plays a big role when we decide which product to buy because we are now immersed in social media every day and there are many influencers who will recommend products and show us the appearance, functions, features, etc. of the products in the form of videos. This can greatly affect our judgment.

十、Success

Your professor is teaching a class on success. Write a post responding to the professor's question.

In your response, you should:

- express and support your personal opinion
- make a contribution to the discussion in your own words

An effective response will contain at least 100 words. You will have 10 minutes to write it.

Professor

As the world becomes increasing complicated, young people are required to be versatile to achieve success in their life or career. What is the essential abilities for young people to have?

Tom

I think the ability to plan keeps us from losing ourselves in endless tasks. As is known to all, today's young people have to deal with far greater number of tasks than people did in the past. If one lacks the ability to plan, he would drown in tons of jobs because things keep popping out all the time. Taking a modern college student for example, he usually has plenty of work to do, but time is always pressing. In a short period of time, he may have to handle a term paper, earn extra credits by playing the role as a teaching assistant, and search for an internship program. Under such a circumstance, a good plan can clearly help him allocate his time and energy well, which guarantees an efficient accomplishment of all the tasks.

Jerry

I think self-learning ability is essential because today's society has higher requirements for young people. In some jobs, it is necessary to master a variety of skills to ensure that the work can be completed smoothly. For example, I was an intern in an advertising company before. In a project, I need video editing function, text organization ability and picture design ability. So the self-learning ability is the core ability to keep us getting the job done.

十一、Life Quality

Your professor is teaching a class on life quality. Write a post responding to the professor's question.

In your response, you should:

• express and support your personal opinion

• make a contribution to the discussion in your own words

An effective response will contain at least 100 words. You will have 10 minutes to write it.

Professor

As you know, city governments have a responsibility to improve the lives of residents. In today's class, we're going to discuss the best way for them to do that. What strategy do you think governments should use to improve the overall quality of life of residents? Why do you think it's important?

Maria

I think investing in infrastructure should be the main priority for every local government. This could include things like repairing roads and bridges, expanding public transportation, and improving access to clean water and sanitation. When cities have good infrastructure, it's easier for residents to get around, and new businesses are attracted to the area. They also experience fewer serious accidents.

Tom

While I agree that infrastructure is important, I think that social programs should also be a major focus. The government could invest in things like education, affordable housing, and healthcare, which can help address issues like poverty, inequality, and access to basic needs. By providing these types of services, the government can help improve people's well-being. These are things that everyone benefits from … unlike a road which is only used by people who drive cars.

十二、Society

Your professor is teaching a class on society. Write a post responding to the professor's question.

In your response, you should:

- express and support your personal opinion
- make a contribution to the discussion in your own words

An effective response will contain at least 100 words. You will have 10 minutes to write it.

Professor

Next week, we're going to spend a lot of time in class discussing the positive and negative ways in which companies affect the world around us. Before we start talking about that in class, I want to hear what you think about the topic. So here's a question for the class discussion board: In your opinion, what is the best way for a company to have a positive impact on society?

Sarah

I believe that companies should focus on making their operations more socially and environmentally friendly. While charitable giving can be beneficial, it doesn't address the root causes of serious social and environmental problems. By doing business in more responsible ways, companies can have a more meaningful and lasting impact on society. Moreover, if they attract positive attention from consumers, they could inspire other companies to do the same. That's the only way we can really solve today's problems.

John

While those are very good points, I think that companies should focus on charitable giving. Philanthropy can provide immediate relief to those in need and contribute to the overall well-being of society right away. It could take years or decades for business changes to have a positive impact on society, and most people just can't wait that long.

十三、Health

Your professor is teaching a class on health. Write a post responding to the professor's question.

In your response, you should:

- express and support your personal opinion
- make a contribution to the discussion in your own words

An effective response will contain at least 100 words. You will have 10 minutes to write it.

Professor

Next week, we're going to spend a lot of time in class discussing that the average weight of people is increasing and fitness are decreasing. Before we start talking about that in class, I want to hear what you think about the topic. So here's a question for the class discussion board: In your opinion, what do you think is the most important cause of these problems?

Katie

One of the most contingent reasons for the increase in people's average weight is clearly the unhealthy eating diet they live on. Traditional food using natural ingredients is now being painfully ignored by the masses. Instead, nowadays, the mass-produced one, fast-food, high in cholesterol and chemical additives, seems to be a more appealing option because it saves people time.

Justin

For me, this problem could be attributed to the sedentary lifestyle of people. Idleness is alluring and modern people are too busy with their work to set aside a reasonable amount of time to work out or do physical exercises.

十四、Crime

Your professor is teaching a class on crime. Write a post responding to the professor's question.

In your response, you should:

- express and support your personal opinion
- make a contribution to the discussion in your own words

An effective response will contain at least 100 words. You will have 10 minutes to write it.

Professor

Next week, we're going to spend a lot of time in class discussing an increase in violent crime among youngsters under the age of 18. Before we start talking about that in class, I want to hear what you think about the topic. So here's a question for the class discussion board: In your opinion, what do you think is the most important cause of this problem?

Molly

I believe that this problem could be attributed to violent video games. According to the recent report in Japan, about 80 percent of young children responded TV games or computer games were the most inspiring for them to make crimes. Thanks to advanced technology, young children can play violent games with extremely clear screens. This has drastically encouraged for children's violent behaviors in real world.

Jake

For me，the first reason that can be easily seen is that in modern life，parents almost spend their time on working to earn money. Obviously，there is less time to take care of and supervise their children carefully.

十五、Morality

Your professor is teaching a class on morality. Write a post responding to the professor's question.

In your response，you should：

- express and support your personal opinion
- make a contribution to the discussion in your own words

An effective response will contain at least 100 words. You will have 10 minutes to write it.

Professor

Next week，we're going to spend a lot of time in class discussing that standards of morality seem to be dropping. Before we start talking about that in class，I want to hear what you think about the topic. So here's a question for the class discussion board：In your opinion，what is the best way for government to improve public morality?

Sarah

I believe that government should incorporate public morality into education. By teaching those related courses，students can have a more meaningful and lasting impact on society. Moreover，if they receive a lot of hands-on experience during classes，they could inspire other people to do the same.

John

While those are very good points，I think that government should improve the laws on immoral behaviors. Laws and regulations can provide immediate solutions to those problems and improve the overall standards of morality right away.

十六、Job Hunting

Your professor is teaching a class on job hunting. Write a post responding to the

professor's question.

In your response, you should:

- express and support your personal opinion

- make a contribution to the discussion in your own words

An effective response will contain at least 100 words. You will have 10 minutes to write it.

Professor

In order to succeed in doing a new job, what is the most important ability for employees?

Katrina

I think adapting to new environments is of certain significance. The environment in college and that in the office are never the same. When in college, all students have to do is study. However, when they step into the office, only focusing on their work and ignoring their colleagues won't help them achieve much. Most of the work has to be done with cooperation among coworkers.

Jack

In my opinion, an employee with excellent knowledge will have a better chance of remarkable performance in his line of work. If equipped with rich experience and extensive knowledge, an employee will be more likely to come up with efficient ways to achieve his goals or effective solutions to problems at hand, thereby making his success more likely. For example, when a team is focusing on a marketing campaign, only those majoring in advertising are capable of showing everyone great understanding and brilliant ideas in marketing.

十七、Friendship

Your professor is teaching a class on friendship. Write a post responding to the professor's question.

In your response, you should:

- express and support your personal opinion

- make a contribution to the discussion in your own words

An effective response will contain at least 100 words. You will have 10 minutes to write it.

Professor

Friendship is the gift and fortune for people. What qualities is the most important for a true friend?

Maria

I think that having a small circle of amusing friends around us imparts a deep sense of happiness and well-being. We have all experienced those moments when we，in times of frustration，burst into laughter upon hearing an innovative or refreshing idea expressed in a witty manner by a friend who has a knack for coming up with ingenious jokes. Such jokes can invigorate our sleepy nerves after a long day.

Kevin

Well，I reckon that friends with smart minds and wisdom can assist us on the road to success. It's true that friends with deep insights and wisdom can offer useful advice. Those friends act as teachers，counselors and even families.

十八、Governments' Taxation Income

Your professor is teaching a class on governments' taxation income. Write a post responding to the professor's question.

In your response，you should：
- express and support your personal opinion
- make a contribution to the discussion in your own words

An effective response will contain at least 100 words. You will have 10 minutes to write it.

Professor

People always talk about the use of governments' taxation income. What is the best use for governments spending?

Jennifer

I think the government can increase public awareness of the importance of physical fitness by funding athletics. Along with the rapid development of society, people need to work very hard to guarantee anything close to a decent life, which causes heavy pressure and more unhealthy state. Therefore, it is the government's responsibility to reinforce the healthy condition of citizens. If more sports facilities are built in neighborhoods, the government can help people realize the importance of doing exercise and staying fit and healthy.

Tomek

I agree that the importance of art cannot be overlooked either. The creation of an artistic atmosphere is conducive to cultivating people's tastes. If a society is artistically developed, its people's souls will be stronger and more content.

十九、Ability

Your professor is teaching a class on ability. Write a post responding to the professor's question.

In your response, you should:

- express and support your personal opinion
- make a contribution to the discussion in your own words

An effective response will contain at least 100 words. You will have 10 minutes to write it.

Professor

As modern life becomes more complex, what ability is essential for young people to have to live in this society?

Sofia

I agree that organization and planning are life-long skills, which are necessary to plan for the future. Besides technological complexities, the world is full of economic opportunities, which can bring further confusion and temptation. But there are life goals that are more valuable and meaningful than money, and it is only with planning that young people will be able to fulfill their dreams.

David

I think that in today's fast paced life, young people juggle many commitments and are faced with many distractions, they need to keep awake and find their goals. Only with clear objectives, people could live better.

二十、Technology

Your professor is teaching a class on technology. Write a post responding to the professor's question.

In your response, you should:

- express and support your personal opinion
- make a contribution to the discussion in your own words

An effective response will contain at least 100 words. You will have 10 minutes to write it.

Professor

Scientists have been working to make technology easier and more human-friendly. How do you think technology has affected our lives?

Vivian

I think that the evolution of technology has made communication between people easier. However, it seems to be making human interaction less personal and more remote, thereby disconnecting people from the world. These new methods of communication have removed geographical barriers between people, but have paradoxically increased the personal distance between them.

Karl

I agree, the same holds true of the workplace. Office devices, originally designed to increase efficiency and productivity, have the opposite effect, complicating the workplace as well as making jobs more cumbersome. Admittedly, the employability of office software and devices have liberated people from repetitive tasks and helped them to perform their work more quickly and to a higher standard. However, they have also contributed to the worries and anxieties of those working adults who are not tech-savvy, making their jobs unnecessarily harder.